THE PUPPY
OWNER'S MANUAL

DIANA DELMAR

STOREY
BOOKS

North Adams, Massachusetts

*The mission of Storey Communications is to serve our customers
by publishing practical information that encourages
personal independence in harmony with the environment.*

Edited by Alice Vigliani and Elizabeth McHale
Cover design by Meredith Maker
Illustrations by Jeff Domm, except for page 122, courtesy of Gentle Leader/Promise,
    "The Natural Behavior Management System," Alpha-M, Inc., Minneapolis, MN
Text design by Leslie Noyes and Mark Tomasi
Text production by Jeff Potter, Erin Lincourt, and Jennifer Jepson Smith
Indexed by Word•a•bil•i•ty

The information in this book is true and complete to the best of our knowledge. All
recommendations are made without guarantee on the part of the author or Storey Books.
The author and publisher disclaim any liability in connection with the use of this information. For additional information, please contact Storey Books, 210 MASS MoCA Way,
North Adams, MA 01247.

Storey books are available for special premium and promotional uses and for customized
editions. For further information, please call Storey's Custom Publishing Department at
(800) 793-9396.

Printed in the United States by Banta Corp.
10 9 8 7 6 5 4 3 2 1

Library of Congress Cataloging-in-Publication Data

Delmar, Diana, 1951–
        The puppy owner's manual : solutions to all your puppy problems
in an easy-to-follow question & answer format / Diana Delmar.
            p.   cm.
        Includes bibliographical references (p.).
        ISBN 1-58017-401-9 (pbk. : alk. paper)
        1. Puppies—Handbooks, manuals, etc. 2. Dogs—Handbooks,
manuals, etc. I. Title.
        SF427 .D4144 2001
        636.7'0835—dc21   2001020922

Contents

Dedication

To my family, my friends, and the inspiration for this book — Butch.

Foreword

"Puppy." On one hand, the word brings a smile to your face as you imagine a soft, wiggling, licking bundle of joy that eagerly responds to your affections. On the other hand, you can't ignore what also comes with puppyhood: chewing, maybe barking or biting, and other typical puppy behavior ranging from raiding every trash can in the house to taking the socks right off your feet!

The way you handle these early puppy troubles and training triumphs will set the stage for your dog's behavior for the rest of her life. There are three keys to successfully raising a puppy: a positive attitude, stamina, and most important, preparation. But no matter how prepared you think you are, no matter how many times you seek advice from your veterinarian, and no matter how many dogs your family had when you were a child, you are bound to have an endless list of questions about handling your puppy the minute after you get her home.

Where do you turn? Does the pet store attendant really know which pet bed or food bowl is best for your puppy? Is your veterinarian going to be readily available to answer every question you have about health care? Will you call in a trainer every time the puppy creates havoc in the house? Of course not.

Most of the questions you will have regarding your pup's basic care and training will not be immediately answered by the animal professionals you patronize. You will have to decide on your own how to best confine your puppy while you are out, whether or not to let her sleep with you, how much to walk her, and when to seek the help of a trainer. You'll also have to determine how to go about cleaning up a mess the puppy has made and figure out how to prevent mishaps from recurring. You'll also have the responsibility of ensuring that your new pet stays healthy and that your home is safe for the puppy. You and only you will make the minute-by-minute decisions about your puppy's care.

This is where *The Puppy Owner's Manual* comes to the rescue. It will answer most of the questions that pop up daily when you own a puppy. Written in question-and-answer format, the book is easy to read and understand. Diana Delmar tells you how to establish a puppy-friendly environment and help your puppy form lifelong good habits. She introduces the tools you'll need to train and handle a puppy and then explains their proper, humane use. She supplements her down-to-earth advice with practical advice from leading veterinary specialists.

Whether you already have a puppy or if you haven't yet but are thinking about getting one, *The Puppy Owner's Manual* will provide the information you need to manage — and enjoy — your dog now and far into the future.

— Dr. Jane Fishman-Leon

Dr. Fishman-Leon is a graduate of Cornell University's College of Veterinary Medicine. She was in private veterinary practice for 15 years and has spent over a decade helping people and their pets through radio and television. She is currently the host of Ask the Veterinarian, *a daily television program seen on America's Health Network.*

part **1**

Solving Puppy Problems

Puppy's into Everything

No matter how adorable and affectionate your puppy may be, there will be times when her behavior truly tries your patience. By understanding her needs and applying some practical strategies, you can eliminate or reduce many of those problems. Then both of you can enjoy the pleasures of puppyhood to the fullest!

How can we teach our puppy to stop chewing everything she can get her teeth on?

Chewing is typical, natural, and necessary puppy behavior. You cannot teach her to stop chewing. You can give her the opportunity to chew appropriate items.

Puppies about four months of age in particular are prone to chewing because that's usually when they start teething, and it will take several more months before the teething process is complete. Teething makes their gums sore; chewing helps the teeth break through the gums. Teething is likely to be a major contributor to the chewing problem if the puppy tries to chew inappropriate objects, whether you are home or not.

Other dogs chew because they are anxious about being left alone, which is known as *separation anxiety.* This is more likely to be the cause of chewing if the dog seems to chew inappropriate objects only when you are not home. More information about separation anxiety appears later in this chapter.

To prevent destruction in the house, help your puppy to form desirable chewing habits:

■**Do not give her the opportunity to chew items you don't want chewed.** Do not let her get into the habit of chewing anything she wants to chew. An easy way to do this is to confine her to one room with the use of baby gates. Make sure anything off limits is out of reach.

The kitchen is ideal because it's generally easy to puppy-proof. Baby gates are good because they allow the dog to see out, and some dogs become anxious if they feel too confined. Confining the dog in a cage, or "crating" the dog, is an option that you'll read more about later in this chapter.

Remove all objects you don't want the puppy to chew and destroy, especially from the room where she is confined. *Remove chewable objects before your puppy has a chance to chew them.* If there is a table with wooden legs, cupboards with wooden corners, or molding around the doorway that cannot be removed, apply Bitter Apple or one of the several other chewing deterrents available at pet stores and through catalogs.

■**Provide the puppy with lots of appropriate and safe chewing objects.** Give her no more than three or four at a time, otherwise she may have trouble differentiating the things you give her to chew from other objects. Keep more chewing objects on hand, and rotate them; puppies find a change in chews interesting, just as children enjoy a new toy or returning to a toy they haven't played with in a while.

Easing Sore Gums

Treat teething puppies with something that will ease their sore gums, such as chilled carrot sticks or dog biscuits. Pet stores sell heavy-duty rubber rings that can be cooled in the freezer.

■**Teach the puppy not to chew inappropriate items.** When you are home, sit on the floor and casually place something tempting that she's chewed before, such as a shoe or a pencil, on the floor next to you. As the dog approaches the object, give a firm "No" but provide her with an appropriate chew item instead. Immediately praise her for taking the item offered.

■ **Exercise the puppy before the family goes out!** A tired dog is more likely to sleep than chew.

Wouldn't it be easier to crate my dog to keep her out of mischief?

It might seem easier, but it may not be the best approach. In some cases it could even make matters worse. Crating, or caging, dogs was developed as a method of house training. Caging has also been recommended by some trainers, breeders, and veterinarians as a way to keep puppies out of trouble. Some experts often recommend caging because they fear that if they don't, dogs will continue to misbehave, and their owners will get rid of them or have them euthanized. Unfortunately, bad dog behavior is the leading cause of dog death. Bad behavior needlessly causes millions of dog owners annually to abandon their dogs at shelters, where the dogs are often euthanized. Other owners, unfortunately, find it takes a lot less effort to put the dog in a cage most of the time than to teach the dog how to live out and about the house. Too often, owners don't stop to think that if they spend a modest amount of time training a puppy, they will have many years of satisfying companionship in the future.

Caging is fine if it's used judiciously — for only a few hours at a time, when you can't be there to supervise. Cages do help keep mischievous puppies from injuring themselves while the owners are out. However, caging should not become a permanent way of life for a dog!

In fact, excessive caging can lead to problems. Dr. Nicholas Dodman of Tufts University School of Veterinary Medicine, a well-known veterinarian and pet behaviorist, says, "Some of the worst behavior problems I've seen are in dogs that were crated for long periods of time."

Caging isolates dogs, and isolation is an unnatural state that can result in psychopathology in animals as well as people. The types of problems that can occur in dogs that are excessively isolated include compulsive behaviors such as pacing, tail chasing, and barking. In some dogs, aggression might even result, Dr. Dodman says. Some dogs cannot tolerate any time in a cage at all; they will panic and fight to get out.

It is also true that some dogs really do like their cages and find them quite cozy. Dr. Dodman believes that caging is an acceptable method of housebreaking if used in moderation. It is also handy to have a cage-trained dog if you take your pet on trips where there might not be a safe place to put him when you can't be there. But be aware that some dogs get terribly upset if they are crated, and they soon become miserable.

Information on how to select a safe cage and train an amenable dog to accept the cage, appears in chapter 10, Tools for Controlling Your Puppy.

How can we keep our dog from chewing wildly and scratching the walls when we are out?

Some people think these dogs are spiteful, but they aren't. Dogs don't have the intelligence to be spiteful. Dogs that want to be with you all the time are experiencing separation anxiety. Even more than most dogs, they become anxious when you leave them. Some become frantic.

These dogs need help becoming more comfortable when they are alone, and they need to learn that you will return after you go out. If possible, devote several consecutive days to addressing this problem and plan on putting in time reinforcing any progress you make.

By all means, give your dog attention, but if he ventures off to another corner of the room to nap, let him be; if he doesn't follow you when you leave the room, don't encourage him to come along if it is not necessary. You want him to learn to be by himself, even if it's only in another room.

Next, start conditioning the dog for your absences. First, exercise the dog so he'll want to nap. Make sure he's relieved himself. Then, leave him alone in his space, which may be the kitchen with baby gates up. Don't make a big deal about it, because you don't want him to think that your leaving him is a big deal. For company, leave on the radio or television with voices speaking calmly. Only leave the dog alone for just a minute or two while you go elsewhere in the house or out into the yard. Do this several times throughout the first day. If he remains calm, gradually increase the time you are separated from the dog. Work up to about 10 minutes or so. If it's going well, try it again the next day.

This time, leave and actually go somewhere. Take a walk up the street or take a short ride in the car for about 5 minutes. Again, *gradually* increase the time you are out and the dog is able to stay alone without chewing, working up to perhaps 15 minutes. Over the next few days, *gradually* work up to a couple of hours.

Remember: As you leave and return, it is important to do so quietly. You want the dog to learn that your coming and going is nothing to get excited about. If your puppy has been destructive, don't scold. It doesn't do any good unless you catch the dog in the act, and for a dog with separation anxiety, scolding could in fact make matters worse by increasing his anxiety.

I've heard many owners make statements like: "He chewed the leg on the table because he was mad I left him alone. He even looked guilty when I came home." The expression on the puppy's face has nothing to do with the object he's chewed or with guilt. He's anticipating another scolding.

When a dog backslides, take a step backward in conditioning. *Consider whether you may have jumped ahead too far too fast* — increasing his time alone, say, from 10 minutes to 2 hours instead from 10 minutes to 15 minutes. *Individualize the conditioning process based on your puppy's behavior.*

If you simply cannot devote time to this project, *then you must make special provisions for your dog.* See if a neighbor can provide some "doggie day care" until you can condition the dog to your absence, so he doesn't become so anxious that he tries to tear down the house.

Will caging my puppy make separation anxiety worse?

Some experts believe that caging or crating dogs with separation anxiety will make the problem worse. My experience indicates this is the case. My Boxer, Beau, clearly had separation anxiety and was highly destructive every time I went out. He didn't just limit himself to the occasional shoe; he gutted an entire section of the sofa and systematically ripped off the molding around the kitchen door.

It's no wonder, however. He came from a puppy mill — a place where large numbers of dogs are bred for sale and are housed under less-than-ideal conditions. At the age of eight weeks he had been transported from Arkansas to Maryland, where he was living in a cage in a pet store. He was insecure and anxious and, I think, had had plenty of unpleasant experiences being left alone. When I got him, he was not only anxious but underweight, and in generally poor health.

Following the recommendation of a trainer, I tried crating him. I was told the dog would find the cage a cozy den and that it would prevent him from chewing. Instead, the dog went absolutely wild. He would defecate and step in it (so much for the theory that dogs never foul where they sleep and eat). He would frantically claw and try to bite the crate in his attempt to get out. I got rid of the crate right away, since it obviously wasn't helping the situation.

At the time, I did not know about the gradual conditioning process. But I found he did much better when he was confined in the kitchen with baby gates, which enabled him to see out two doors into other areas of house and to look out the window. It also limited his freedom just enough to help keep him out of major mischief. I left on the television for company. Since my office was near the house, I came home at lunchtime. If I couldn't, I arranged to have a neighbor or my mother come in to let him outside and play with him for a short while.

It took quite a number of months, and as he graduated from the kitchen to the rest of the house, he would behave for days or weeks, then occasionally destroy another item. But eventually he learned to stay by himself and that I would always come home. And instead of staying with me every minute I was in the house, he eventually would go off to take a snooze in the living room while I worked upstairs. He turned out to be a very well-behaved dog.

My point here is that if you have a dog that takes well to a cage and seems to find it comforting, by all means use it for a few hours at a time as need be; but do not force an unwilling and anxious dog into a cage.

Separation Anxiety

Dogs with separation anxiety need some extra effort and special care from their owners. For me, repairing any damage that Beau did until we worked things out was well worth the effort. He guarded my house and gave me countless hours of laughter, and we shared 11 wonderful years of companionship.

Is there a way to keep my puppy from digging holes in the middle of the yard?

There are a number of reasons that dogs dig. Some want to bury bones (or dig them up). Others dig out a shallow hole because it's a cool place to rest on a warm day. For other dogs, it's just a way to expend pent-up energy. If your puppy has been home sleeping all day while you are at work, he's probably expending energy.

I'd first try a vigorous play session as soon as you turn him outside. Fetch is good because it requires the dog to run around a lot. If he then starts digging, redirect the behavior. If he's burying a bone, for instance, take it to an acceptable digging place, perhaps in the back of the yard, and encourage him to dig there. When he does, reward him with verbal praise. Or, when he starts digging in an unacceptable place, "herd" him to an acceptable place. If he returns to the spot in the middle of the lawn despite your attempts to redirect his behavior, try a firm "No" to discourage him, and show him again where digging is acceptable.

If you do not want him digging anywhere, conduct the play session, then take him back into the house and distract him with more play or a favorite chew. By not giving him the opportunity to form the habit of digging, he may stop the behavior if he's given other outlets for his energy.

Dogs that dig in the yard may have too much pent-up energy, indicating that other forms of exercise are needed.

My puppy gets into the trash can at every opportunity. How can I get him to stop?

Don't expect him to! It's too much to ask of a young puppy and even an older dog to stay out of the trash, especially if there are scraps of food in the trash can. However, it is important to deal with this problem because it's not just a nuisance, it also could be hazardous. The dog could swallow sharp bones, resulting in internal wounds, or cut his mouth on the sharp edges of discarded metal cans.

The cheapest and easiest solution is to keep the trash can out of reach. This is an example of one way that you can change the environment to accommodate your puppy. You want the dog to forget about the trash can and all the temptations it has to offer. Put the trash can up on a counter or into a cupboard. If you can't do this, try a tall model trash can with a tight lid. This is likely to keep out a small dog, but not necessarily a large and determined one.

As you train the puppy and he learns to obey, especially the command "No," you can begin to teach him to stay away from the trash can when it's within his reach and you are there to supervise. Reward him when he listens.

There are gadgets you can buy in catalogs to deter the dog. One looks like a big plastic mousetrap that goes off when the dog gets near the trash. Or, you could sit in waiting with a water gun and squirt the dog when he goes near the trash. These are forms of adverse, or negative, conditioning. Generally, negative methods of conditioning a dog should be reserved for situations when all else fails.

Protecting the Trash Can

To help make the trash can uninteresting to dogs of any age, keep it free of tempting food odors. Freeze food scraps, such as leftover chicken, in a plastic bag; then toss them when you take out the trash for garbage collection.

Can I break my puppy's habit of playing with rolls of toilet paper?

This typical puppy behavior is fun for the puppy! The puppy is also getting lots of attention as you chase her around the house trying to rescue the roll.

When you are in the bathroom using the paper, ask the dog to "Sit" and "Stay" if she has learned those commands (see chapter 11, Training Basics). Use the time as a training opportunity. Reward her with generous praise — "Good girl!" and a friendly pat on the head. If she doesn't have a clue yet what these commands are, simply close the door to the bathroom when you are using it to keep her out, and when you are not in the bathroom, store the roll of paper in a place that is out of reach of the dog. As the dog matures, she will get into the habit of playing with the toys you provide for her and out of the habit of stealing toilet paper.

Rewarding Good Behavior

When you're trying to teach a puppy to behave, it's generally preferable to do so by rewarding the dog for good behavior. Why? Being rewarded is a positive experience; being scolded isn't. Dogs certainly need to learn the meaning of "No," but try to choose your "Nos" wisely and don't overuse them. If you say "No" too often, some dogs will start ignoring the word altogether.

Try to form the habit of distracting the puppy away from "bad" behavior and toward appropriate behavior so you have an opportunity to reward her. Say your puppy keeps trying to grab a sponge you're using to wipe up the mess on the floor she just made by knocking over her water bowl. Instead of yelling "No!" you might walk away from the spot and get one of her favorite chews that is likely to occupy her. Ask her to "Lie down," and when she does, pat her on the head and give her the chew. You've created a situation that enables you to reward her for doing something good, instead of yelling at her for being bad.

Laundry day is impossible! The puppy runs off with dirty clothes.

All dogs seem to love the smell of dirty clothes. Be flattered: The clothes smell like you. Keep dirty clothes in a hamper that is inaccessible to the dog.

When the dog tries to steal clothes as you're sorting them on laundry day, consider it a training opportunity. Ask her to "Sit" and "Stay," or to "Lie down" and "Stay," as you complete your chore. Praise the dog for obeying. Keep some treats in your pocket to reward her.

Remember that puppies have a short attention span. Don't expect her to "Stay" for a long time. As you repeat this exercise, though, you'll notice the dog is able to "Stay" for greater periods of time. One of my neighbors taught her Golden Retriever to "Sit" and "Stay" while she ironed.

If the dog still manages to run off with a valuable item, the fastest way to get it back and prevent the dog from damaging it is to distract the dog with something more tempting. Call the dog to you, and offer her a favorite treat. If you're lucky, she'll drop the item to get her treat, and you'll also be practicing the "Come" command. I've found that when nothing else works, ringing the doorbell usually does!

If none of these suggestions work, put up a baby gate in the doorway of the room where you are sorting laundry. The puppy can be near you and see you, and you can keep an eye on her, but she'll be less likely to make sorting laundry an impossible task.

I have scolded him hundreds of times for it, but my puppy just won't stop chasing my cat.

This is a tough behavior to change, and it will take time. It's instinctual for dogs to chase cats. For this problem, distraction seldom works.

Put the dog on his leash, and take the dog near the cat. When the puppy lunges toward the cat, tell him "No!" and immediately ask the dog to "Sit" and "Stay." Reward him immediately with a small treat. If the cat comes around, but you don't have the puppy on a leash and you can see he's ready to bolt after the cat, tell him to "Sit, stay!" The second he begins to listen to you, reward him with generous pats and verbal praise. These exercises will have to be done over and over and over for days, weeks, or even months.

Now, you obviously will not be able to stop the puppy from chasing the cat every single time the two encounter each other, so until you get this behavior under control, take measures to prevent the puppy from terrorizing the cat — and to keep the puppy from being injured if the cat claws in self-defense. Use baby gates to separate the two. For example, if your cat likes to spend time in the upstairs of the house, put up a baby gate at the foot of the stairway or keep the puppy confined in the kitchen with baby gates so he can see out and also get used to the cat wandering around. (Don't forget to put the litter pan, food, and water for the cat in his own part of the house!)

You hope that the presence of the cat eventually will become commonplace and less interesting to the dog — although at the age of two, my dog still occasionally chases my two old cats if I'm not there to intervene with a "Sit, stay!" and a reward.

Let Them Work It Out

There's one other possible solution to this problem. If your puppy isn't too aggressive and the cat isn't terribly upset at being chased by the dog, see if they can work it out on their own — but only if you are there to make sure things don't get out of hand. If the cat gives the puppy a good swat or two, the puppy may leave the cat alone in the future. If there's any chance the cat might seriously claw the puppy, especially in the eyes, or that the puppy might injure the cat — or if you think your cat is feeling terrorized by the dog — this approach isn't a good idea. Don't try this if you have a dog with prominent eyes, such as a Pug. Eye injuries occur more easily in these dogs and can be serious.

How can we encourage our old dog and new puppy to get along?

New puppies often want to play; old dogs don't and, in fact, may not like puppies much at all. Help your older dog adjust to the puppy. This will take time, however, since a new puppy in the house is a big change in your older dog's life.

Without realizing it, you probably are giving the puppy more attention than the older dog, just because puppies need lots of attention. When people visit your house, they probably pay lots of attention to the puppy, and the old dog gets a perfunctory pat on the head.

First, be sure to keep your older dog on the same schedule he's been used to. Also protect your older dog from the puppy. In other words, don't let the puppy jump all over him and roughhouse if the older dog isn't interested in playing this way. Keep the two separated if you must.

Then try to make the presence of the puppy a positive experience for the older dog. Spend some time alone playing with or just patting the older dog, then have someone else bring in the puppy. You stay with the older dog, and with your tone of voice, act as though the entrance of the puppy is a very pleasant event. Pat the older dog some more, and give him some treats. You are trying to get him to associate the new puppy with positive attention from you. If you can, do this several times a day for several days. See if he doesn't improve.

How can I keep the puppy off the furniture?

Provide the dog with a comfortable bed of his own. Encourage him to lie in the bed, and reward him for doing so. When he gets up onto the furniture, there is really no need to scold while you are teaching him. Instead, take the dog to his bed, tell him "Down," and reward him. Repeat this process as necessary.

You might want the dog and his bed elsewhere when you are not home, but when you are home relaxing in your favorite chair, place the dog bed close by. Letting the puppy be near you and patting him on the head from time to time will help reinforce the good habit of lying in his own bed.

If you have valuable furniture and you want to make sure the dog stays away from it when you cannot supervise, block off access to the room that contains this furniture by closing a door or by using a baby gate.

Another approach is to use a product such as a "Scat Mat" or "No-Go-Mat," which can be purchased from pet catalogs or in some pet supply stores. These devices, which deliver a low electric charge to pets, can be placed on furniture. But these mats aren't cheap: They cost from about $60 to $80. There also are training aids that emit a loud sound if the pet jumps onto furniture; these cost about $30. Both types of devices provide negative instead of positive conditioning. Always try positive conditioning first, and give it a really good try before using negative conditioning.

Consistency and Repetition

Consistent instruction and repetition are the key to successful puppy training. If you scold your puppy for getting up onto the sofa one night, then let him up onto it the next, you can't expect him to stay off the sofa when you are not at home. Nor can you expect the puppy to stay off the sofa if you've only tried to redirect his behavior one or two times. If you are consistent and repetitive, you'll be amazed at how rapidly your puppy catches on.

How can I get my puppy to leave me alone?

When you have a puppy that paws at your arms or jumps up on your lap constantly, you very likely have a bored dog that needs lots more exercise than he's getting. Before you sit down to relax or work, try a vigorous walk and a play session with the dog. Different dogs require different amounts of exercise. For some, 10 to 15 minutes a couple times a day, or one long romp around the yard, is adequate; but other dogs may require far more exercise.

Also, make sure the dog isn't trying to tell you that he's hungry or needs to relieve himself when he's "at you." He's totally dependent on you, so make sure his basic needs have been met before expecting him to settle down.

Keep in mind that if you put in, say, one-half hour or even an hour with your puppy taking care of his needs before you focus on work at your desk or enjoying a quiet read, the puppy will be less likely to disturb you when you don't want him to.

When you do sit down to work or relax, teach the dog to lie down on his bed near you and "Stay." Reward him for obeying. Do not expect him to stay put for long at first. Give him a chew toy that you know he likes — peanut butter smeared on a bone or stuffed into a marrow bone is a favorite with most dogs. More ideas appear later in this chapter.

The other option is to put the puppy in his "space," such as the kitchen, after you exercise him. He may rest quietly there in his bed while you work or read.

If you know you have a hectic day coming up and that you won't have the time to provide the dog with the exercise he needs, consider hiring a professional dog walker or pay a trusted neighborhood teenager to walk the dog.

Yet another option for handling a very active dog is to get him a playmate. If you can manage the cost and don't mind the basic chores involved with two instead of one dog, this can be an excellent "cure" for an active but bored dog. Beware, however, that if you are having specific behavior problems with your puppy, such as chewing or barking, getting another dog won't correct these problems. A second dog is something to consider if the problem is simply that your dog could use a playmate.

Dogs can be taught to lie down and stay quietly by their owners, but it takes time and patience.

Is medication ever appropriate for misbehavior in puppies?

You may have read that it is now possible to control a dog's behavior with drug therapy. But Dr. Dodman believes that this is virtually never a solution for a puppy, unless there is a medical condition causing the problem. The kinds of medications used to treat dog misbehavior are psychotropic drugs that affect chemicals in the brain, but they tend to be used in older dogs. Some of them are the same drugs that are used in humans to control problems such as anxiety.

Most puppies — including the ones that seem to be in constant motion and into everything — are not hyperactive. They are perfectly normal, but their owners don't realize just how active puppies can be.

The only time drug therapy might be indicated for puppy misbehavior, says Dr. Dodman, is when a behavior problem becomes excessive or extreme and does not respond to behavior modification therapy, or when the owners, for some logistical reason, cannot implement effective behavior training. In an older puppy that is dominant and aggressive toward its owners, for instance, Dr. Dodman says he might consider drug treatment as a short-term measure until the owners can get a handle on the problem and implement behavior therapy.

Otherwise, what these puppies need is some attention from their owners. "These dogs need limits set. They need to be taught to do the right thing," he says.

Irrational Behavior: Hypothyroidism?

If you have an older puppy that is demonstrating extreme, irrational behavior and no amount of behavior modification seems to help, consider hypothyroidism, Dr. Dodman says.

"This syndrome in young dogs is just now coming to light. Unlike older dogs with hypothyroidism, which have poor coats, a pot-bellied appearance, and act sluggish, veterinarians are finding that young dogs with hypothyroidism can demonstrate a completely different picture," he says. Some are hyperactive; others are anxious; some develop compulsive behavior, such as continual licking of themselves; and others may even show signs of aggression.

Hypothyroidism should be considered in animals with one or more of these behaviors when there seems to be no explanation for the cause. "Experts usually can tell how a dog got the way it is," Dr. Dodman says. For example, if a dog was previously treated with cruelty, it would be no surprise if that dog were to become aggressive out of fear. But if a dog was bred and raised under ideal conditions and demonstrates this kind of behavior, the behavior would be considered irrational, he explains.

The one or two thyroid tests usually performed to identify thyroid deficiency in dogs, Dr. Dodman cautions, may not detect hypothyroidism in these cases. Owners should ask their veterinarians to obtain a full thyroid panel. (The cost of a full thyroid panel varies depending on where you live and which lab your veterinarian uses, but it generally runs about $60.) In puppies with behavior problems arising from hypothyroidism, treatment with a synthetic thyroid hormone will, in many cases, reverse the behavior in just days or weeks, he says.

How old should our puppy be before we start giving her free access to the whole house?

Many people provide a "space" for their puppy, such as a roomy kitchen. Barricaded by baby gates, the puppy can stay in her bed while they are out so that she doesn't get into mischief or hurt herself while they are away. How long to continue this pattern depends entirely on your dog. If she is very well behaved in the kitchen, and generally a calm dog not prone to inappropriate behavior, you could try giving her access to one or two more rooms now. Don't turn her completely loose in the house yet; having too much freedom too soon is how puppies get into trouble. Instead, block off a larger space with baby gates, such as the kitchen and the family room instead of just the kitchen. Or close doors in the house so that she only has access to one larger area. Then try leaving her alone only for 10 or 15 minutes the first few times.

If this goes well, keep giving her that same amount of increased space for the next two or three weeks when you go out. Then gradually increase the area that is accessible to her, and the amount of time you leave her alone. If giving her more freedom does not go well, backtrack — reduce the space she's given.

Very energetic, mischievous dogs may need to stay in their "space" every time you go out throughout their puppyhood. And although dogs are considered puppies until one year of age, many of them act like puppies for the first two or even three years of life! If they are getting adequate exercise and attention when not in their space, are not left in their space for excessive periods of time, have plenty of room to move around in their space when they are confined there, and do not soil in the house when you leave them (indicating they are getting outside as often as they need to), it's fine to restrict them in their space for several hours at a time for as many weeks, months, or years as you need to.

Our large-breed puppy destroys every toy and chew we get him. Are there toys that would last?

A greater problem than the destruction of toys is the possibility that the dog might bite off and swallow a piece of a toy or chew. Often, swallowed foreign objects pass safely through a dog's system, but they might end up causing an intestinal blockage instead. That's why it is imperative that every toy and chew you give your dog be sturdy enough, and that when there's ever any question that a new toy or chew won't hold up, you should only give it to the dog when you are present to supervise.

Flimsy vinyl or plastic toys or balls with squeakers and bells in them will not hold up. Avoid them. The squeakers and bells also pose a serious choking threat if the dog swallows them.

Many dogs enjoy carrying around stuffed toys. The kind made for children usually have button eyes and noses that can be chewed off and pose a choking hazard. There are similar toys made for dogs without buttons, or you can easily make your own. Just use sturdy material, and sew up the sides very tightly so the puppy can't rip them open and eat the stuffing.

Kong toys, which are made of heavy rubber, are very durable. They can be packed with small dog biscuits or bits of cheese to encourage the dog to play with them. Used in this way, they will keep a puppy busy for quite a while as he works to get out the treats.

Rawhide is a type of chew that I would categorize as a "maybe." If your dog has powerful jaws, he'll be able to chew off little pieces of even the sturdiest rawhide bones. If you give your dog rawhide at all, do it when you are present to supervise. And buy rawhide so large for your dog's size that chewing off pieces is difficult.

Of the various rawhide products available, pressed rawhide is harder and less likely than the nonpressed variety to become soft and tear into pieces, although my dog eventually chews the ends of these into slimy, thin pieces. I either cut off the thin ends (while they are still soft — it's nearly impossible once they harden again) or confiscate the chew and throw it away.

Pig ears and calf hooves are popular dog chews. However, I had a large dog that once bit off and swallowed a sharp piece of a hoof. Luckily, he threw it right back up. That was the last time I gave him that kind of chew. The small dog I have now manages to chew pig ears into slimy pieces and once started to choke on one, so he's not allowed to have any more of these. He seems to delicately chew on calf hooves and does not get off any pieces, so he's allowed to have one occasionally, with supervision. My experience demonstrates the importance of evaluating every chew you give your dog to determine if it is safe for your puppy.

Nylon bones, such as the Nylabone, are among the safest chews on the market. They come in a variety of shapes and sizes, but be sure to get one large enough so the dog can't get the entire bone in her mouth, which again could present a choking hazard. Some dogs find plain nylon bones boring, so buy a flavored one or dip the plain version in something tasty like chicken broth, or smear it with peanut butter. Some nylon bones become pitted or very rough with use, and then they can scratch a puppy's face, so toss them when they become worn and replace them.

Never give dogs chicken bones or any other type of bone that might splinter. More on protecting your puppy appears in chapter 6, Keeping Puppy Safe.

A Special Treat: Marrow Bones

A very special treat that dogs enjoy is a marrow bone. Buy them from a butcher or in the meat department at your grocery store. They cost about 15 cents each. Select them carefully: Avoid those cut at an angle that have sharp, boney material inside; opt instead for marrow bones that are cut straight across and are circular, with soft marrow inside.

Boil them for about 20 minutes, then cool. Scrape off any sharp gristle on the outside that the dog might otherwise chew and ingest. I give the dog one bone, and freeze the others for later use. Dogs love to work at getting out the marrow. Once the marrow is gone, you can fill the bones with peanut butter. Marrow bones also can be filled with dry dog food made into a mush with water; freeze the bones with this filling, then thaw them a bit before giving them to the dog. If the marrow bones get grungy after your puppy eats out the treat in the middle, put them in the dishwasher. Toss the bones when they show signs of wear.

"Bathroom" Blunders

(and Other Messy Problems)

Housebreaking doesn't have to be difficult. By establishing a routine that accommodates both your puppy's needs and your own daily schedule, it's possible to incorporate him into your family's lifestyle without sacrificing your carpets and furniture or his "right" to act according to animal instincts. It just takes some patience, knowledge, and repetition on your part.

We're house training our puppy. How do we make sure she doesn't go in the house?

When you're trying to housebreak a new puppy, even those that usually use the backyard sometimes go in the house. The solution: *Never give the puppy the opportunity to go in the house.* Set aside several days devoted to housebreaking her, then plan on reinforcing what she learns. Start by taking her out *very often* at first — at least every two hours. This will make sure she has plenty of opportunity to go outside, not inside. It also will give you an idea of just how often she needs to urinate and defecate.

Be sure that you take her out at the key times that puppies tend to go: after sleeping, after eating, and after playing. When you are too busy to supervise her in the house, keep her in her "space" (see chapter 10, Tools for Controlling Your Puppy) or on a leash with you so she can't go off and relieve herself in the house.

> "The goal is never to let your puppy have a chance to go in the house."

Puppies usually don't have to go as often overnight, when they are sleeping, but there are exceptions. Try taking the puppy outside just before going to bed and very early in the morning. You'll quickly be able to determine if she can hold her urine all night. If not, you may have to take her out once overnight, at least for a while, so she doesn't go in the house. If you're finding she has to defecate overnight, try adjusting her feeding schedule. If you've been giving her a feeding at 9 P.M. and she has to poop at 3 A.M., try feeding her the last meal either earlier, so she can poop before bed, or much later, so she doesn't have to poop again until morning. I do not recommend withholding water from puppies before bed; I think if they are thirsty, they should be able to drink and that owners should accommodate their need to urinate, too.

If your puppy manages to sneak off and go in the house when you are home, and *you catch her in the act,* issue a sharp "No!" Then immediately, but calmly, take her outside to show her where she is supposed to go. Do not act angry as you take her outside; you have issued a correction, but you want her to associate going outside with something positive, which is your jolly, pleasant mood. If you don't catch her in the act, don't bother scolding. It's a useless gesture because she won't be able to figure out why you're scolding her.

When you have to go out and leave the puppy at home, take her outside before you leave, make sure she goes, then leave her in her "space." Be sure to allot enough time to accomplish this task. Usually, puppies sleep when left alone in their "space" and won't have to go quite as often; but during the initial intensified training period, try to arrange your schedule so she is taken out every two or three hours. Remember, the goal is to never give her the chance to go in the house. You may have to enlist the help of a relative or neighbor to take her out if you must be away for more than a few hours.

Owners who consistently stick with this plan will find that their puppies learn to go outside very quickly. Some puppies can learn in just a day or two. That doesn't mean you can stop taking her outside often;

compared with older dogs, bladder control in puppies under six months of age is not as good. Puppies definitely need to go out more often. But once you can see that she is forming the habit of only going outside, you can try letting up a bit on the frequency of outdoor trips. You'll have been able to figure out, for instance, that she needs to go outside first thing in the morning; after she eats, plays, and naps; and otherwise, maybe just a time or two more. If you give her the opportunity to go outside as often as she needs to go, you'll have few if any accidents indoors.

We want to paper train our dog because we are out all day. How do we do this?

Paper training a puppy remains an excellent method of housebreaking a dog, especially for owners who cannot be home enough to get a puppy outside as frequently as needed. Remember, puppies do not have the bladder control that older dogs do, and they need to urinate more often.

To paper train a puppy, leave her in her "space," such as the kitchen with baby gates, and cover the entire floor with newspaper. After she gets

If you are paper training your puppy, you will eventually need only a small section of newspaper covering the floor. But don't make it too small!

used to going on the newspaper, gradually start reducing the area you have covered. She'll probably use the same general section of newspapers on the floor, anyway. But to encourage her to go in one place, leave a piece of newspaper with a urine stain on it, and if you can stand to, with a little remaining smear of poop. (You can cover the dirty sheet of newspaper with a clean one.) The odor will encourage her to continue using the newspaper.

Eventually, you should only need a small section covered with newspaper. If she backslides and uses the floor, increase the area covered again and start over; next time, reduce the space covered with paper more gradually. Some puppies will try to use the newspaper but get their feet too close to the edge, their back end on the floor, and miss the newspaper. This is a common mishap. It should be of no concern, and certainly it is not a reason to scold the puppy. Just clean up the mess well enough to eliminate odor so the dog doesn't think the bare floor is where she's supposed to go.

> **Paper Training**
>
> Puppies that are paper trained may urinate and defecate on newspaper whether it's on the floor or not, so keep newspapers up and out of reach if you don't want your puppy to use them. If you forget and your puppy does "go" on newspaper somewhere other than in his space, don't scold. He's only doing what you have taught him to do.

Our puppy came to us paper trained. How do we convert her to going outside?

Plan to make the transition over the course of several days, using the same method described in the first question and answer in this chapter: take her out often and do not give her the chance to go in the house. First, however, take a piece of newspaper soiled with urine and feces, and put it outside where you want her to go. It will give her some inspiration. Indoors, keep her with you on a leash so she does not have an opportunity to wander off and go in the house. She will form the habit of going only outside.

If you have to go out and leave her alone for more than a few hours, you may want to put the newspaper back down in her "space" while you're gone. Remove it when you will be home to take her outside often.

How do we use a cage to housebreak the dog?

Dogs generally don't like to urinate or defecate where they sleep. The theory is that if puppies are kept in a cage or crate when you aren't there to supervise, and it's just big enough for a sleeping space, they won't go in the cage, nor will they have a chance to go in the house.

Puppies that are crated must be taken outside very often, just as if you were housebreaking without the use of the crate. Initially, they should go outside every couple hours. It is not kind or fair to expect a puppy to "hold it" for long periods of time.

If you must keep your puppy in a cage for more than two or three hours at a time, buy a cage large enough to provide a sleeping space at one end and a newspaper-covered "bathroom" at the other. Or, have someone come in to take the dog outside.

Some crating advocates advise against giving dogs water when they are crated so they don't have to urinate. If you want to use a crate, I think it's preferable to provide water so they can quench their thirst when they are thirsty. Adequate water is crucial to the well-being of all animals. Some bowls come with an attachment that can be screwed on to the cage, preventing dogs from spilling the water.

Going on Command

Teach your puppy to recognize a word or phrase that means "Go outside and do your business." You can do this by using the same word or phrase each time you take the dog outside to urinate or defecate. I say "Make outside." Reward the dog for going with lots of verbal praise. After he starts to urinate, for example, quietly praise him with "Good boy! Good boy!"

Dogs that learn to associate a word or phrase with doing their business eventually will learn to go on command. This comes in very handy when you want to make sure the dog has gone before bedtime, or before you go out and leave him alone at home.

Watch also for your puppy's "sign" that he has to go outside. Many dogs will stand at the back door or paw at the door. Others will come to you and yap or jump up and down on their front paws. I heard once about a dog owner who trained her puppy to jingle sleigh bells hanging from the doorknob as his cue that he had business to attend to in the backyard!

By taking your puppy outside often, and by never giving him the chance to go in the house, he'll learn to do his business outside.

Are doggie doors a good way to help house-break a puppy?

For older dogs, they can be very convenient if you have the kind that connects to a secure, fenced-in backyard, primarily because dogs can go out to do their business when they need to without you having to let them out each time.

However, a doggie door is not a good idea for a puppy, especially a very young one. You still need to housebreak him first — he won't know he's supposed to go outside to do his business just because a doggie door is there. In addition, puppies tend to be mischievous and need to be supervised when they go outside. They may try to escape from the yard to chase other animals. Before letting my dog use a doggie door, I'd want him completely housebroken, fairly well trained, and well past the puppyhood stage. I'd want to be sure he's not the type of dog that wants to roam.

Beware of doggie doors that come with solid, slide-in fixtures that can be used to shut off the door to burglars. If a dog goes outside — say, you let him out through a different door — and tries to run back in through the doggie door, he could break his neck. Also beware that doggie doors can provide an entrance for burglars when a slide-in fixture isn't in place. My family had one years ago, and we used it to get into the house when we locked ourselves out!

Can a dog be trained to go in the house in a box, like a cat?

If you have a very small breed female dog, yes. In fact, it's a very convenient option for many owners. If your puppy is paper trained, simply put some newspaper with urine odor on it in the box you want the puppy to start using. For very tiny dogs, you may want to begin with a paper box with one side cut out to make it easy for the puppy to get in. Later, graduate to a plastic litter box like the ones used by cats.

You can continue to use layers of newspaper, or shredded newspaper, which soaks up urine pretty well if you have enough newspaper down. Some owners have trained their dogs to go in kitty litter; there are now sand-like brands available that enable you to scoop out the stool and flush it, even though it has the sand on it. This kind of material is probably going to be messier than newspaper, because the puppy is likely to kick some of it or a lot of it out around the box. Some puppies may not like the feel of kitty litter, and you may have to stick with newspaper.

Using an indoor box might be possible with a male if he squats to urinate. Be careful, however, not to be fooled. Most male puppies don't start to hike their legs until they reach puberty; some hike their legs and then return to squatting if they are neutered, but not all do. You could think you have a "squatter" on your hands and find him hiking his leg in the house later on.

How small a dog needs to be to go in a box in the house will depend somewhat on your tolerance for cleaning up after the dog. Many pet owners have cats weighing about 15 pounds that use a litter box in the house. The smaller the dog, the less the mess.

My housebroken puppy started having accidents as soon as the weather outside became frigid.

If your dog is small or has a short coat, he may not want to stay outside to finish his business. He's simply uncomfortable in cold weather. Some dogs also refuse to go out in the rain. Buy him a sweater or raincoat, as appropriate.

Put his coat on, then bundle yourself up, too, and take him outdoors. Bring a few treats in your pocket. Act like going outside is great fun. Make it a positive experience. If he runs back to the door despite your presence, put him on a leash. Encourage him to run and jump around, which will increase the likelihood he'll have to urinate or defecate. Give him a treat as soon as he shows interest in playing and stops trying to run back to the house.

You'll have to stay outside with him long enough to get him to go. As soon as he starts going, quietly praise him by saying, "Good boy, good boy!" (If you say it too loud, he may stop.) As soon as he's done, reward

Doing "Business" in Cold Weather

Here's a tip for making it easier for a puppy to go outside in miserable weather. But whether you can use it depends on the design of your house, your yard, and the size of your dog. Pull up a patio table right next to the back door. If the dog is small, you can teach him to go underneath the table.

During the blizzard of 1996, when snow drifted over four feet high in my backyard, this is the only place my dog could go for days! Pick up stools immediately when temperatures are very cold. If you don't, they'll freeze to the ground or the patio and will be almost impossible to remove until temperatures rise again.

him with a treat, more lavish verbal praise, friendly pats, then take him back into the house. Repeating this routine *many times daily* for several days will be necessary. The goal here is to avoid giving him the opportunity to go in the house and to make it habit again to only go outside. You also want him to know that as soon as he goes, he gets to come back into the house.

Once you feel that going in the backyard has again become routine for the dog, try encouraging him to go outside on his own. Start this on a day when the weather is nice.

Backsliding is to be expected. When it happens, you'll have to resume taking him outside again.

Could the presence of our new baby upset our puppy and cause her to have accidents?

A change in the household, such as a houseguest or a new baby, could be enough to prompt some dogs to break training. Backtrack several steps. Return to the house training methods you used before that worked. If you initially trained your dog by taking her outside often and never giving her the chance to go in the house, resume that routine. When you weren't home, you may have had her confined in the kitchen with baby gates, safe chew toys, food, water, and with newspaper down that she could urinate on. If this was the case, do it again.

As you resume training methods, be sure to make them positive experiences. Taking her outside should be fun; confining her to the kitchen should not be punishing, but pleasant. Instead, do whatever you can to make it possible for her to do the right thing — urinating outside — and reward her.

If you catch her in the act of going in the house, issue a moderately sharp "No!" followed by a quick trip outdoors. But don't be too severe; it could backfire by making her a nervous wreck about urinating, which could result in more accidents. If you find a wet spot in the house but were not present when she made it, scolding won't do any good.

Make it a point to see that the dog's usual routine is disturbed as little as possible and that she's getting as much attention as she's used to. If you have a new baby, this sounds impossible, but there are ways to include her and make the baby's presence less disruptive to the dog's life. Encourage your dog to come with you when you go to check on the baby, or to sit and stay next to you while you change the baby's diaper. When you are interacting with the baby, talk to the dog, too. Make the presence of the baby a pleasant experience for the dog. The same approach should be used when there are guests in the house.

Urinary Tract Infections

A break in house training can be a sign of a urinary tract infection or obstruction. Other signs of an infection include straining — squatting like she has to go but doesn't — dribbling urine, pain on urination, more-frequent-than-usual urination, or blood in the urine. If there is no apparent reason for a dog to break training, and especially if there are any signs of urinary tract infection, call your veterinarian.

How can I keep my male puppy from "marking" when we go visiting?

This is an entirely different problem from a break in house training. Your dog wants others to know he's been there, and he's doing that by marking the spot with urine. It's instinctual.

When you go visiting with your dog someplace indoors, keep him on a short leash and watch him carefully so he doesn't have the opportunity to mark. He'll be more likely to mark if you take him somewhere where there are other animals present. You'll have to be on your toes, because a male can hike his leg and "squirt" pretty fast. Use the "Sit" and "Stay" commands (see chapter 11, Training Basics). If he does start to mark, a sharp "No" is in order, followed by a quick trip outdoors.

Some dogs will continue trying to mark no matter how diligent the owner is about training. I have a dog that was a marker; he squirted urine every time I took him anywhere there were other animals present, and he marked places in our own house where the cats hang out. He even marked one of the cat beds while the cat was sleeping in it! The solution for us was neutering. It reduces the level of hormones that may contribute to the problem. Amazingly, my dog never marked again from the day he was neutered, and he was neutered later than usual — at about 16 months of age, a time when his marking behavior was well established. I know of other owners who found neutering was the solution to marking behavior.

Neutering, however, isn't a guarantee that marking will stop, nor will it work alone. Neutering must be coupled with training, because marking can become a habit, even if instinct initiated the behavior. Whether you plan to have your dog neutered or not, avoid giving him the chance to mark and correct him when he does, if you catch him in the act.

How do we get urine odor out of the carpet?

This is an important task to accomplish. Urine odors must be removed, because if left, they will encourage the dog to go again in the same spot. This also holds true for male dogs that are marking territory with urine.

If the urine stain is fresh, a vinegar and water solution works well and is very inexpensive. I mix one part vinegar to three parts water. Keep some of this solution handy in a small spray bottle. If urine has really saturated the carpet, you may have to soak the area with the vinegar and water mix, then soak it all up with a thick towel. After it completely dries, sniff the spot to see if there is any lingering odor that requires further treatment, although dogs may be able to smell an odor that we can't.

If an odor remains, or if it's an older urine stain, try a product called Outright Pet Odor Eliminator, which can be used on carpets and upholstery. It is sold in pet stores, some veterinary clinics, and pet catalogs. The product is advertised as a "beneficial bacteria and enzyme formula" that eliminates odors arising from organic waste, such as pet urine, as well as vomit and feces. It can be used on "all water-safe surfaces," including upholstery, carpets, mattresses, and even plants. It is not supposed to stain carpets and is nontoxic.

This product must be mixed with water. After application, you must keep the area covered with a damp towel until the odor is gone, which takes as long as a day.

The price of this product may vary depending on where you buy it, but one pet catalog sells a concentrated, eight-ounce bottle for under $6 and a 32-ounce bottle for about $13 (plus shipping and handling). One part of the concentrated solution is mixed with five parts water, so it's quite cost effective. Many pet stores and veterinary clinics also sell this and similar products.

Preventing Repeat "Accidents"

Sometimes, puppies will gravitate toward the same "bathroom" spot despite your best cleaning efforts. If this is the case for you, be sure to not only meticulously clean the spot, but take action immediately to keep the puppy away from the spot. You could block it with furniture or spray a deterrent, such as Bitter Apple, on a towel and cover the spot, which will make it an unpleasant place for your puppy to "visit."

Our puppy gets excited and wets herself, especially when we have company. What can we do?

Like marking territory, this kind of urination is different from breaks in house training. It is called *submissive urination.* She's saying she's beneath you (or your guests). You might say this dog needs to improve her self-esteem. Keep in mind that very young puppies do not have well-developed bladder control, and dogs often outgrow this behavior as they mature.

In the meantime, take this advice from Dr. Bonnie Beaver, author of *The Veterinarian's Encyclopedia of Animal Behavior:* "Owners must become deliberately less threatening." Avoid directly staring at the dog, squat on the floor with the dog instead of standing over her, and encourage her to come to you instead of reaching for her. Make your voice high-pitched, soft, and coaxing. Do not punish a dog for submissive urination; it will only make the situation worse, because the dog is already submitting to the owner, Dr. Beaver warns in her book.

Protect your puppy from guests who may inadvertently be aggressive. Explain the puppy's behavior, and ask that they not approach her.

It might be useful to ask a cooperative friend to help. Have the friend come to visit, sit on the floor, and quietly talk with you, at first ignoring the dog. If the dog has not urinated, have the friend speak a few words very quietly and gently to the dog, but from a distance. If the dog still hasn't urinated, repeat the exercise the next day; if things are still going well, ask your friend to pay just a bit more attention to the dog and get just a little closer. You could have more sessions, each time gradually increasing the visitor's contact with the dog. If the dog urinates, backtrack a step or two in your approach, or just give her more time to mature.

Although my puppy is housebroken, she always defecates in an "inconvenient" place.

If your dog defecates on the edge of a neighbor's lawn or the sidewalk, it can be difficult to clean up. Identify a place as close to your home as possible where it is appropriate for her to go (and easy to clean up), and take her there first each time you go out. Mulched ground or ground with loose dirt makes a good doggie bathroom; it's easy to lift off stool. Start going to this place at a time when she is likely to go, such as after a meal, and try to keep her around this spot until she does her business. Make your visit to this place pleasant: Play with her, and reward her when she finally goes.

It may take some persistence and patience on your part to get her to go just where you want her to the first few times. Eventually, however, she will develop the habit of going in this place if you do not give her the chance to go elsewhere.

If she does have a mishap on the way to her outdoor bathroom, there is no need to punish her — she is going outside of the house and that's great. But be sure to clean it up! When my dog was very little, on more than one occasion I had to go back with a bottle of water to rinse a sidewalk because picking up the stool just wasn't enough. This will keep the neighbors from complaining.

What's the best way to pick up and dispose of dog feces in an urban area?

Many communities enforce laws requiring dog owners to pick up their dog's stool from the curb or other community property. There are numerous products made just for picking up dog stools, but I've never spent a cent on one of them. My newspaper comes in sturdy, long plastic bags, which I save and use for dog stools. I keep one or two of these bags in my pocket each time I take my dog out for a walk; after the dog goes, I insert my hand in the bag, pick up the stool, turn the bag inside out, and tie it off. If your newspaper doesn't come in plastic, you could use grocery store plastic bags — but these can get little holes in them, so I'd double them up.

In some areas, feces are not supposed to be put into the trash. Check with other dog owners in your neighborhood to see if they know where it is and isn't appropriate to dispose of dog stools in the area. I've found that complaints from the garbage service are unlikely if the stools are in a tied-off plastic bag, and then placed into another, larger garbage bag. The double-bagging method helps contain odors.

What's the best way to dispose of dog feces in the backyard?

You can buy a "Doggie Dooley" system, which basically is a large bucket made of heavy plastic or galvanized steel. You dig a hole and sink the bucket into the ground. The device comes with a lid and an enzyme "digester," which is a product you put into the bucket. It helps break down dog stool, which then drains off into the ground. My parents have had one of these in their yard for years, and it's a convenient place to dispose of stool.

However, in my own small yard, it didn't work because I have clay soil and poor drainage. The stool never drained out. After a rain, I had an overflowing mess in the backyard. If your yard is large enough, you could bury the stool. Covering stool with lime also helps; it eliminates odor. But keep your puppy away from lime — it can burn paws.

Is it normal for a puppy's stools to be soft and messy?

Soft stools are difficult to clean up. You may even have to wash the dog's behind after he goes. Although you may wonder if your puppy is sick, generally the reason for this is that what goes in comes out. A diet primarily of wet, canned food can sometimes result in a soft, messy stool. Digestive upsets from sudden changes in diet also can cause a messy stool.

If you are feeding wet food, you could try another brand that seems to have less moisture in it than the brand you currently are using. Or, introduce a good-quality dry food recommended by your veterinarian. Introduce any new food gradually (over the course of about five days) to prevent digestive upsets. Begin by mixing in a very small amount of dry food with the dog's wet food, then increase it until the stool is of a manageable consistency. If your dog will eat dry food, this can become his sole source of food. Some dogs prefer dry food moistened with warm water to soften it slightly. There are many nutritious dry foods available, and they yield a nice, firm stool that is very easy to clean up, even if you've added water.

Diarrhea

Diarrhea can be caused by a variety of factors. A sudden change in diet is one cause. Moreover, milk can cause diarrhea in some dogs. Another cause is worms or intestinal parasites. Dogs sometimes eat garbage and other substances that can irritate their gastrointestinal system. Infections are yet another cause of diarrhea.

If your puppy has one bout of diarrhea but no other signs of illness, and his stool returns to normal, he's probably fine. Diarrhea that persists or contains blood warrants a trip to the veterinarian. So does even one bout of diarrhea that is accompanied by other signs of illness, such as loss of appetite, lethargy, or vomiting.

If you cannot get your dog to eat some dry food mixed in with wet food, try adding rice to the wet food. If the dog eats this, cook one big batch and freeze it in individual portions, which can be microwaved and then added to the wet food as needed.

If your dog has been eating dry food and has a loose stool, or if he's on wet food now and adding dry food doesn't firm up the stool, call your veterinarian for help.

What's the best way to clean up after a puppy who has diarrhea in the house?

This isn't pretty, but it's how one experienced dog breeder cleans up this kind of mess — and she has German Shepherd dogs, so the mess is substantial!

Remove any excess diarrhea sitting on top of the carpet. Take care not to rub any in. *Let the rest completely dry.* Otherwise, you'll just smear the mess further into the carpet. Block off the area to keep people and the puppy away. After it dries, go back with a smooth-edged, dull knife — one that won't tear carpet fibers — and scrape the carpet clean. Vacuum. I recently tried this method on a commercial carpet I have in the basement, and it worked like a gem. I used a rough sponge instead of a dull knife to remove the dried stool; it came right out in dry flakes. Follow with a carpet cleaner. There are several on the market now that are advertised to remove pet stains and odors.

Preventing Carpet Discoloration

To prevent discoloration of carpets when your puppy has an accident, avoid feeding any food that contains dyes, especially red dye. It will leave stains on some carpets that are difficult if not impossible to remove.

Our puppy has a foul odor around her rectum, unrelated to bowel movements. What's wrong?

Dogs have two scent glands, or anal sacs, on either side of their rectum underneath the skin. In wild animals, they are used to mark territory. In most dogs, the anal sacs are routinely emptied when the dog defecates, and the owner never even notices. Sometimes, however, the sacs empty when a dog is upset or excited. I've had dogs that occasionally release anal sacs while they sleep. These are the times you'll notice the odor, and the only comparable smell I can think of is the odor of skunk. When this happens and you notice the foul odor, wash and dry the dog's rear end. A little vinegar slightly diluted with water may help eliminate the odor from carpet or fabric. Or, try a carpet or fabric cleaner.

Anal sacs can become clogged and infected. You'll know when this happens because the dog is likely to scoot on the floor, dragging his rear, or will act uncomfortable when he defecates. A discharge around the rectum, especially if it is bloody or contains pus, also indicates an infection. If this is the case, contact your veterinarian right away.

I've found that a diet that produces a firm stool seems to facilitate routine emptying of anal sacs.

Should I ban our puppy from sleeping under the covers with our daughter? He gets the sheets dirty.

Puppies shed, snort, and generally make a mess, yet children love to have their puppy sleep with them, even if it means mom or dad has to change the sheets daily. There are several possible solutions. If your puppy is used to sleeping in his own bed when he's in his "space," and there is ample space in your daughter's bed, put his bed in your daughter's bed and see if he won't stay there at night. Or, put down an old sheet or towel (one that is easy to remove and wash) over a section of your daughter's bottom sheet and train the puppy to lie on it instead of elsewhere.

You could train the dog to lie on an old sheet, towel, or quilt placed on top of your daughter's bed covers. Dogs that want to stay under the covers generally are seeking warmth. If you decide to train the dog to sleep on top of your daughter's bed covers, you may want to put a light cover over him to see if that keeps him from crawling under the covers.

Training a puppy to sleep in a different way will take some persistence. If the dog migrates back to a place you don't want him to be, your daughter will have to keep putting him where it is acceptable for him to sleep. It will be easier if you teach your puppy the "Down" and "Stay" commands (see chapter 11), and teach your daughter to use them.

Our dog sheds heavily. How do we get the hair off our furniture?

The easiest way is with a powerful vacuum, such as the handheld Dirt Devil. But even a powerful vacuum will not always remove animal hair that gets worked into a textured material.

I've spent quite a bit of money ordering products from catalogs that are supposed to remove worked-in hair, and none of them work well. In fact, as I write this paragraph, I just received delivery of yet another device; this one looks like a window squeegee and says on the label that it "removes even matted-in hair from furniture." I ordered it to get out pet hair that was worked into my office chair. Guess what? It is no more effective than any other contraption I've tried! The hair comes out slowly and only with considerable effort. Pet hair removal rollers (which are nothing but large sheets of heavy-duty masking tape on a roll) help a little, but they still don't make this an easy chore.

A better solution is to cover the chair with a throw that can be easily washed. Or, you may prefer to train your puppy not to get on furniture that is just too difficult to clean.

chapter 3

Play and Exercise Annoyances

Many people don't realize how much exercise healthy, growing puppies need. By giving her plenty of appropriate outlets for that boundless puppy energy, you can make your puppy's playtime or exercise time a fun experience as well as an opportunity to develop good habits. It's also a time when you learn more about your puppy and deepen your relationship with her.

My new puppy learned to "fetch" right away, but he won't let go of the ball so I can throw it again.

One way to get the ball back is to "wait out" the dog. If you try to get him to drop the ball, he'll think this is part of the game because he is getting attention from you by keeping the ball in his mouth while you try to get it away from him. Instead, sit quietly, waiting for him to get bored enough to drop the ball. Then work on teaching him to "Sit" and "Stay" (see chapter 11) before you pick up the ball and throw it again. This also will help ensure he doesn't grab at the ball the same time you do and nick your fingers with his teeth. Eventually, the dog will learn that if he puts the ball down and waits a second, you'll throw it again for him.

Here's another method. Get three or four balls. When he brings back the one you've thrown, show him the second ball. Start to throw it, but don't actually throw it until he drops the first ball, which he's likely to do because he'll be excited with anticipation of chasing the ball that's in your hand.

Some owners teach their dog a command, such as "Out," that means "Drop the ball" (or whatever the dog has in its mouth). You might start introducing this word whenever your dog puts down the ball, and see if he doesn't readily learn this command.

How can I stop my puppy from biting my hands with her sharp little teeth when we play?

If you've ever watched puppies play with one another, you'll see that they often use their mouths. Now, you're the puppy's "pack," and she's engaging in the same kind of play behavior with you. It's entirely normal. She needs to learn, however, to be gentle with her mouth.

To do this, trying issuing a moderately loud "Ouch!" every time she hurts you with her teeth, then walk away and ignore her for several minutes. You don't want to give her attention for this undesirable behavior, and she'll learn that hard play bites are unacceptable. If she touches your hand with her teeth *gently*, a gentle "No" is in order, but not a severe scolding. Return to play activity, and do not let her form the habit of "mouthing" your hand.

Here's why you don't want your dog to use her mouth on people, even if she's gentle about it: If your dog ever accidently touches a stranger with her mouth, and that person is an "overreactor," your dog could be accused of biting even if her action was completely innocent and harmless.

Our puppy is a lovable little guy, but sometimes he gets rough with our children.

Some puppies run and knock children over and stand over them if they are on the ground. Make sure your children are not encouraging this behavior. If they are jumping, running, and rolling on the ground with the dog, the dog could easily become overexcited and caught up in "rough and tumble" play. The dog is treating the children as if they were part of his "pack," and you can't expect him to know otherwise.

The children must learn that they have to command the dog's respect; to do that, they must be controlled when they play with the dog. In other words, no running, which encourages the dog to chase them; also, they should not get down on the ground with the dog, which encourages him to "pounce" on them.

If they are old enough, teach the children how to practice basic obedience commands with the puppy after he learns them. This will help the dog respect the children, and it will teach him to obey if the children issue a command.

Very young children should not be left alone with the dog because they might encourage inappropriate play behavior, and the dog might accidentally injure them. Don't give your dog a chance to be "bad."

If these suggestions do not work and the dog seems to get rough with the children even though they have not instigated the behavior, you need to enlist the help of a professional trainer to assess the situation and recommend specific training.

Aggressive Behavior

Anyone with a puppy that demonstrates aggressive behavior, such as snarling or vicious growling or nasty lunging at people, should immediately seek the help of a professional trainer. However, only use a trainer who is recommended by your veterinarian, by someone on staff at your local humane society, or by other dog owners. Be sure the trainer uses positive and not negative reinforcement.

I read that it's a bad idea to play tug with dogs. Why?

A number of trainers advise against playing tug because they believe it promotes aggressive behavior. On the other hand, many owners routinely play tug with their dogs because their dogs love it, and they've never had a problem. I think the answer depends entirely on your dog.

If your dog shows no signs of aggression when playing tug or at any other time, and if he's not an especially large or powerful breed, playing tug is probably fine.

By the way, most dogs do growl when they play tug. They do this as they pull against the tug toy or object. If you are not sure whether the dog is growling playfully or being aggressive, then don't play tug.

It's difficult to walk my dog because he wants to sniff instead of walk.

It's natural for a dog to sniff and track. Dogs originally bred for tracking, such as certain hound dogs, will be especially prone to this behavior. Sniffing scents left by other dogs outdoors can actually be positive; it gives your puppy inspiration to urinate and defecate, which you want him to do when you take him outside.

Start out your daily excursions in a place where the dog can find interesting smells and where it's acceptable for him to do his "business." Let this be the place and time that you allow him to relax, sniff around where he wants, urinate, and defecate. When you take him to this spot, use a word such as "Okay" and a tone of voice that conveys, "At ease; do what you want" (on leash, of course).

Then let him know it's time to move on. Use "Heel" if he already knows that command, but if not, the combination of something like "Let's go!" and your movement away should get him to follow. You'll probably have to tug a bit. Immediately take him to a place, such as a sidewalk, where there are unlikely to be so many attractive things to sniff. Encourage him to keep going so he doesn't form the habit of stopping just anywhere he likes.

Sometimes, a dog is more likely to move on if you walk backwards, facing the dog and vocally encouraging him to come along. If necessary, carry treats the puppy likes in your pocket and use them to help keep the dog moving.

The goal here is to make it the puppy's habit to sniff, probably urinate and defecate, then move on. This takes practice. You'll also be training the dog to go in one place. That's a plus in urban areas, where you do not want the dog just going anywhere.

As you both learn to walk nicely together, vary the walking portion of your outing so it doesn't become boring for you or the dog. Visit the "bathroom" place, then set out in a different direction each day. Walking in different places with your dog also exposes him to different distractions, which helps him learn to obey in a variety of situations.

Your puppy may resist continuing his walk if he smells something interesting. Try walking backwards, facing the puppy, and vocally encouraging him to come along.

Just how much exercise does my puppy need?

For average dog owners, exercising the puppy is important because it will reduce the incidence of behavior problems. Puppies also need some exercise for optimal growth and development, whether they get their exercise by walking on a leash or romping in the house with the kids.

The breed of dog can give you some clues about exercise requirements, but the needs vary among individual dogs of the same breed and there are exceptions to every rule. Dogs originally bred for working, such as the Siberian Husky or the Chesapeake Bay Retriever, generally require lots of exercise. A friend of mine had a Labrador Retriever that at the age of 14 still expected long daily walks in the park and an occasional swim in the creek, despite severe arthritis.

For smaller companion dogs, such as the Pekingese or the toy Poodle, an occasional walk and romp in the house may suffice. Bulldogs (commonly called English Bulldogs) often require little exercise and some have respiratory problems, making much exercise at all difficult. But there are exceptions, and some Bulldogs require quite a bit of exercise to keep them out of mischief.

The best way to determine how much exercise your puppy needs is by observing his behavior. If he is generally fit and not overweight, is

How to Help an Energetic Puppy Expend Energy

- **Put your dog on a leash, and take him for brisk walks.**
- **Play fetch.** Use a ball, flying saucer (such as a Frisbee), or other toy. A note of caution: If you are playing "Frisbee," do not encourage your puppy to jump into the air. This could strain delicate, growing joints. Dogs require gradual conditioning for this type of exercise. And don't play fetch with sticks or twigs. They can injure your dog's mouth. I had a dog that bit off the tip of his tongue this way!
- **Play hide and seek.** Throw the dog's ball, and as he goes to fetch it, hide in another room. Do not frustrate your dog or "spook" him by hiding for more than a few seconds. Make a little noise if necessary to help your dog find you. This game is simply another way to interact with your puppy and get him moving around for exercise.
- **Buy your dog a beach ball if you have a fenced-in yard.** Most dogs love chasing it around, and some become quite adept at hitting it into the air with their noses.
- **Give your puppy something to get wild with!** I've used cardboard boxes (with no staples or other dangerous parts) and the cardboard tubes that come inside wrapping paper. Try these with your dog and see if he doesn't exhaust himself tearing them up. It makes a bit of a mess, but it's easy to clean up. (There is the risk this could lead the dog to freely play with any boxes or rolls of wrapping paper you have around the house, but for me, it's proved to be a simple, economical way to help him expend a lot of energy. I just keep boxes and wrapping paper that I don't want him to have up and out of reach.)
- **Turn a plastic laundry basket upside down over several of your puppy's favorite balls, toys, or treats.** He'll get lots of exercise trying to recover the loot. If he can't figure out how to flip over the basket and get out his toys after several minutes, though, do it for him. Otherwise he'll become frustrated and then fed up and won't want to play this game again.
- **Take your puppy for a swim.** On a hot day, many dogs love a romp in the water, and most are good swimmers. Of course, make sure your dog can swim by testing out his abilities in a small pool where you can easily rescue him if needed.

    If you don't have a backyard swimming pool, a small, inflatable children's pool might suffice. Try to buy one that won't be too easily punctured by the dog's toenails. Where I live, I have nowhere to put such a pool, so I fill up a huge pan with water and let the dog splash around, or I take him to a large, fenced-in yard and turn on a rotating lawn sprinkler; he has loads of fun and gets lots of exercise chasing the water back and forth.

calm while in the house, and is not developing behavior problems such as inappropriate chewing, he's probably getting enough exercise. If he seems to be into everything in the house and is developing inappropriate behavior, he probably needs more exercise.

Beware, however, that *puppies must be exercised carefully.* Although some vigorous exercise is good, it should not be rough or prolonged, which could injure growing bones and joints. It's acceptable for your dog to be panting lightly after an exercise session, but the dog should not be on the verge of collapse! Some ideas for exercising your puppy appear on page 43.

I walk my puppy, but have no yard where he can run. How can I provide more exercise?

You can provide your puppy with lots more exercise indoors. See the ideas for exercising puppies in the box on page 43. Fetch, hide and seek, or ripping up an old cardboard box are all games that can be played indoors as well as outdoors.

If you are concerned that you will disturb neighbors who live below by letting the puppy romp indoors, talk to them before they have a chance to complain. Explain that you don't want to bother them, and inquire if there is a time they are unlikely to be home when you could let the dog make some racket.

Provide a little extra exercise for your puppy by taking him along with you whenever possible. This will also help socialize the dog. If you have to go down the hall to collect the mail or into the basement of your apartment building to put in a load of laundry, put the dog on his leash and bring him along. If your hands are full, tie the leash to your waist (but don't let the leash hang so slack that you could trip on it or step on it and flip the dog).

Another option is to consider getting your puppy a playmate (if you can handle the added health care and feeding expenses, and don't mind walking two dogs). Two dogs usually will entertain and exercise one another.

Can my puppy be trained well enough to obey me off-leash?

If you live in a condominium or urban area, the only exercise your dog usually gets is when you walk him on his leash. You can tell he'd like to run or romp off-leash in a nearby park, but letting any dog off a leash in any area where there are cars in the vicinity is a serious threat to his life. Yes, dogs can be trained to obey off-leash quite well. However, even an older, highly trained dog cannot be expected to obey every command 100 percent of the time. For any dog, some temptations are just too hard to resist, such as a rabbit scampering into the path of a car. A professional trainer might be confident a dog is trained well enough to resist temptations. I know of few average dogs of average pet owners that are trained this well.

In many neighborhoods, dog owners have turned certain areas into play yards where their pets romp off-leash together. This is a great idea if the areas are fenced in. Others are not. Dog owners say that the attraction of other dogs seems to be enough to keep them all together and prevent them from running off, but it's no guarantee. I don't think it's worth taking the risk.

Instead, try to think of a friend or relative with a fenced-in yard where you can take your dog to run freely. It would be nice if this person had a dog of their own that could play with yours. Be sure to clean up after your dog if he defecates in the yard so you'll be welcome back in the future!

To provide your dog with a little more freedom on your walks, buy a very long leash. Leashes are available in a variety of lengths; some are 50 feet long. Some come with a handheld device that enables the leash to expand and retract automatically as your dog moves around, and they have a "brake" so you can stop the dog quickly. A long leash will enable your dog to move around a lot more on your walks. You can even play fetch outdoors with your puppy if the leash is long enough.

Keeping Paws Clean

Try to keep your puppy from walking through motor oil, or on roads or sidewalks covered with chemicals or salts intended to melt ice. If she does, wash her feet after bringing her into the house. You don't want her licking these substances off her feet because they might make her ill, and some of them can burn her paws.

One more note is in order about dogs off-leash. In many urban areas, there are laws requiring dogs to be on a leash at all times. In some areas, the laws even limit the length of the leash allowed. Check with local authorities to see what the rules are in your area.

How can I stop my puppy from attacking my shoes, my socks, and even my bare feet?

It's not uncommon for puppies to go for shoes, especially those with tassels or shoelaces. Some dogs persist in this behavior long after other undesirable puppy behaviors have ceased. This behavior warrants a sharp "No" and then a distraction with a favorite toy or chew. If he obeys, reward him with pats and verbal praise.

If you aren't getting anywhere after trying this approach several times, try a sharp "No" and *immediately* remove yourself from the dog by walking away from him and shutting a door behind you, if necessary. Repeat the exercise. You want to get the message across that the dog gets no attention for this behavior, but that he receives praise when he is around feet or shoes and doesn't go after them.

You could use the same method when a guest is in the house (assuming the dog only wants to go after the guest's shoes); or you could put the dog on leash and keep him with you, asking him to "Sit" and "Stay," and then rewarding him as he listens and stays put.

An alternative method if nothing else works is adverse conditioning. Put on an old pair of shoes or socks and apply a deterrent such as Bitter Apple. If the taste is unpleasant enough to him, he should leave shoes and feet alone in the future. If you have cooperative guests, you could apply one of these substances to a napkin or cloth and place it over their shoes.

Some trainers advise using a toy water gun for adverse conditioning. This works for some dogs, but not for others. Mine, for instance, loves water and thinks getting squirted is great fun. Another method of adverse conditioning commonly recommended is shaking coins in a can.

If all these methods fail and your puppy is attacking guests' feet, scold the dog and put him in his "space." However, scold the dog at the sight of the offense, but don't continue scolding him as you put him in his space; you want him to associate his space with something pleasant.

Will neutering discourage a male puppy from mounting when he gets overexcited?

Many male puppies do this when they play, mounting people's legs, stuffed toys, and even pillows on the sofa. It can be especially embarrassing when you have company. There is no guarantee that neutering will work, but it does stop the behavior in some dogs. By the way, some female dogs, spayed or not, also demonstrate this behavior and will "hump" pillows or stuffed toys.

In *The Veterinarian's Encyclopedia of Animal Behavior,* Dr. Bonnie Beaver explains that inappropriate mounting can be a common behavior in juvenile males nearing puberty. Excitement, such as having visitors in the house, can be enough to trigger the mounting of inappropriate objects. Inappropriate mounting is a behavior most commonly demonstrated by males that have not been neutered, which provides a strong argument for castration as the treatment of choice, Dr. Beaver says.

Talk to your veterinarian about neutering the dog. Generally, experts advise against neutering male dogs before they have reached puberty, because it may impair bone development. The ideal age to neuter a male may vary depending on the breed.

In the meantime — and whether you have the dog neutered or not — take measures to prevent this behavior from becoming an obnoxious habit. When the dog tries to mount, quickly move him and distract him with his favorite toy or chew. Dr. Beaver notes that exercising a dog can help prevent inappropriate mounting behavior, so try taking your pet on a long walk or have a vigorous game of fetch with him in the backyard before guests arrive.

Online Pet Information

If you're a dog owner with a computer and subscribe to America Online, try out the Pet Care Forum. It's a fantastic resource for all types of information about pets. You can communicate with other dog owners and even get advice from veterinarians to complement information provided by your own puppy's doctor. It's worth checking out. You can access it simply by going to "keyword" and typing in "pets."

Isn't it better to keep a puppy in the backyard where he can exercise?

Some people feel that keeping a puppy outside is healthier for the dog, but leaving a dog alone in the backyard, especially a puppy, can be a recipe for disaster. The puppy will be subjected to the elements, such as unpredictable temperature changes, that could make him miserable or make him sick. If it's warm weather, he will be bitten by mosquitoes, pestered by gnats, or stung by bees, which can be especially dangerous if your puppy turns out to be allergic to these pests. It's also too easy to put the dog out and forget about him.

Moreover, there is the very real risk that your puppy could be stolen. And, contrary to common belief, dogs left alone outside seldom exercise themselves. They are more likely to sit around and be bored. If you have a fence, the dog might find a way over it by climbing it if he's large enough, by digging under it if he's small enough, or by finding something to help him get over, such as a log pile.

There is another potential problem. Dogs left alone in the backyard most of the time do not become socialized, which makes them more likely to act aggressively toward anyone venturing into the backyard. To raise a friendly, nonaggressive dog, you have to allow him to be with people as much as possible. Your puppy won't learn to become a good house pet if you don't keep him in the house most of the time.

Dogs left alone in the backyard seldom exercise themselves, usually become bored, and are likely to be bothered by pests.

If you insist on making your puppy spend time in the backyard alone, do not attach him to a cable, especially if he wears a collar. It is not that difficult for a dog, especially a puppy, to become hung up and hurt his legs or even strangle himself. Instead, buy a pen specifically designed for outdoor use. This is sturdier than any pen you might use indoors. As with a fence, you'll have to make sure he cannot dig out under the sides and get out, that the sides are high enough to prevent escape, and that he can't climb the sides and get out. There must be a secure gate and lock.

Dogs that are outdoors a lot must have a thoughtfully designed doghouse that is kept clean and that will protect them from the weather. A floor raised off the ground is recommended. There must be comfortable bedding inside and a door flap to protect the dog from wind when he's in the house. Books with special advice about building or buying a doghouse should be consulted. You can find them in bookstores or in catalogs that sell pet products. Doghouses also can be purchased ready-made, and some are available through pet catalogs.

The house must be located on ground with good drainage. The footing around the house should be of a material that won't be uncomfortable for his feet. Concrete is sometimes recommended, but unless the kennel area is shaded, it could become too hot for a puppy's feet in summer. The kennel should be within reach of a garden hose so you can clean up after your puppy easily.

Even with a doghouse, there should be shade over part of the pen area to protect your puppy from hot sun, access to plenty of water and food, and safe toys and chews for entertainment.

Ideally, dogs in the backyard should have a companion dog for company!

Even if you do all this, I would only pen a puppy outdoors for short periods of time — an hour or two daily when the weather is pleasant — and only if your puppy seems to like being in the pen. Remember to check on him often!

chapter 4

Eating-Related Irritations

Of course you think of your puppy as another member of the family, but he's still an animal as well. Begging, growling, gobbling food, vomiting, refusing to eat, and eating weird things are problems you may encounter, but you can deal with them if you know how. You'll also want to make sure you feed your puppy properly to assure he is well nourished.

Every time we sit down to eat, the puppy begs for food. How can we stop her?

If you never want your puppy to beg from the table, you must never feed her from the table. To break the begging habit that has already ensued, try completely ignoring the puppy. This is tough to do, but be determined not to pay one bit of attention to the dog. Carry on with your meal just as you would if the dog were not present. You may have to do this for several meals until the puppy gets the message that she gets nothing when she begs. If you've been feeding her from the table, it may take even longer. Once the dog stops begging for food and is quiet throughout your meal, praise her as soon as you have finished eating.

If the dog continues to beg after you've diligently ignored her for three or four meals and you are convinced this method isn't working, switch tactics. During your meal, confine the dog to the kitchen, family room, or some other place where she has a comfortable bed and some favorite chews. Make it a pleasant, not punishing, experience.

If you want to give her any leftovers, do it after you take your plates to the kitchen. Feed the scraps from the dog's bowl only.

Some owners occasionally give their dogs a piece of food from the table. I'm one of them! However, I've trained my dog to lie down while I eat, and after I finish, he gets a little scrap of food. The price I pay for this is occasional begging.

When we're eating dinner, our puppy asks to go out by standing at the door, but it's really a ploy to get us to play.

Your dog has learned that going to the back door gets your attention, and that's good for house training purposes. To stop the dog from interrupting your meal, however, try this: Before you sit down to eat, make sure the dog has gone outside and done his "business" so you are sure he doesn't really have to go outside. Begin eating. When he goes to the back door, call him to you in an encouraging, friendly manner, then ask him to lie down near you. Give him one of his favorite chews. Praise him occasionally with a pat on the head.

The goal here is to make it an enjoyable experience for him to be quiet while you eat. Continue to be responsive when he goes to the back door at other times, and praise him for going outside when he should.

Alternatively, you could use baby gates to confine the dog to a room where he has a bed and chews to keep him occupied while you eat (after making sure he's relieved himself outside). Get him out of the habit of going to the door during your meal. After several meals with the dog confined, let him into the dining room or kitchen while you eat, and have him lie down quietly. Reward him for obeying. If he starts going to the door instead, backtrack a step and resume his confinement while you finish your meal.

Our puppy will do just about anything to get to our food. How do we stop this behavior?

I've known dogs who are so bold they even jumped onto the dining room table while their owners were eating. These dogs really need obedience training, especially with "Down" and "Stay" (see chapter 11). Until you get the training well under way, put the puppy in her "space" while you eat so she can't develop the habit of hopping onto the table for food.

When you start working on "Down" and "Stay," it's important to give her a chance to obey so you can reward her. The minute she lies down, reward her before she has a chance to get up and disobey. Then work on "Stay," using the same technique, and gradually build on the time she is able to obey this command.

Once you feel you are making progress, use the commands to try and get her to obey while you are dining. Before you have your meal, make sure she's been fed and relieved herself outside. Ask her to lie down and stay on her bed in a place that's visible, but away from your table. Reward her with dog treats when she listens, but don't do it by feeding her from the table. Have treats set aside and take them to her. If she gets up and comes near the table, a sharp "No!" is in order. Walk her back to her bed, and repeat the commands. Do it over and over. She'll catch on eventually.

Just how often should I feed my puppy?

Experts say that because puppies are growing so rapidly, they require about twice as many nutrients as adult dogs. If they are under six months of age, many breeders advise free feeding, or leaving food out and available to the dog at all times. The food left out should be dry food, since wet food can spoil; but offer fresh canned food in addition to the dry food at least a couple times daily, when you will be there to remove any the puppy does not eat. You can mix the wet with some dry at these times; the dry food helps keep the stool firm and easier to clean up. If you do not want to free feed for some reason, feed your puppy three or four times a day until she is six months of age.

Once she is six months old, you can begin feeding her twice daily. If her appetite is good and she is not overweight, you could continue leaving some dry food in a bowl for her when she is home alone. I think puppies should have access to food whenever they are hungry. Weight problems usually do not start until after puppyhood, when dogs have stopped growing and receive more food (and often get less exercise) than they need.

My puppy growls if anyone comes near her when she's eating. Is she going to be a vicious dog?

This behavior doesn't necessarily mean the dog is vicious, but it is aggressive behavior that needs to be nipped in the bud. If the dog is a small breed or a young puppy, and you're sure she can't seriously injure you if she were to bite — and she shows no other signs of aggression — you probably can handle this problem yourself. (Always keep your face out of the way, however.) Here's how:

1. *Start by making the dog eat her food out of your hand.* Slowly give her two or three small bites this way. Then have her eat a small amount of the food in your hand, but with your hand in the bowl. Make her eat a couple meals this way.

2. *Next, start out again by having her eat from your hand, then from your hand in the bowl,* but add another step: Place a small amount of food in the bottom of the bowl. Let her eat several bites, then quietly remove the bowl. If she growls, issue a sharp "No!" Keep the food bowl up on the counter for a few minutes and go do something else in the meantime. Repeat the exercise from beginning to end until she no longer growls when you remove the bowl.

3. *After you've gotten this far, repeat the entire process again,* and then try giving her just a pat or two on the back gently while she eats. If she accepts this, tell her "Good girl!" If she doesn't and starts to growl, issue a very sharp "No!" and again remove the food *immediately.* Go do something else and ignore her for a while, then repeat the procedure.

    Your goal is to get the dog to the point where she will tolerate your removing her food, as well as touches from you when she takes a bite of food from the bowl. You want the dog to learn that for growling, she gets something unpleasant — which is no food or attention — but that if she eats without growling and snapping, she gets more food, pats, and praise.

4. *After you've gotten the puppy eating for you without growling,* have any other adults in the house perform the same exercise if possible, as well as any children old enough to do so safely, calmly, and quietly. You'll have to use your own judgment about whether your child is mature enough, but I'd say a child should be at least age seven or so. Reinforce your success by repeating the exercise periodically with the dog.

5. *If all this goes well, have a friend or neighbor come around* the dog when she is eating. I'll tell you a story that explains this bit of advice. I know of a dog that doesn't growl at anyone in the family who comes around when he eats, but he acts vicious if anyone outside of the family comes around during his mealtime. This is unacceptable, and it's probably only a matter of time before the dog ends up biting someone. This is why I would advise also teaching your puppy to accept nonfamily members around her at mealtime. She must learn that growling over food is inappropriate no matter which human is around.

Bloat

If you have an older puppy, especially a large-breed dog, beware of a condition called *bloat,* or *overeating syndrome.* Gas and fluid build up in the stomach, and the stomach can actually twist, causing a life-threatening situation that can only be corrected by surgery. Dogs with bloat will look as though they have abdominal stress; they may drool and vomit, although nothing comes up. If your dog ever has any of these signs, get him to a veterinarian immediately.

Bloat can occur in small dogs but usually is seen in large male dogs, and especially big dogs that eat a large meal, drink a lot of water, and then exercise vigorously.

Bloat usually is not seen in puppies and tends to occur in grown dogs. However, it's a good idea to form habits now that will prevent your dog from ever developing this condition. If you have a large-breed dog, plan on always feeding two smaller meals instead of one large one throughout the dog's life. Then wait at least one hour after your dog eats before letting him exercise or play vigorously.

It is very important that you put some extra effort into obedience training your dog. Otherwise she might begin to show signs of aggression even if there isn't food around. I'd enroll her in an obedience class. By taking action early when signs of trouble appear, most owners can control and eliminate behaviors that could turn out to be serious problems down the road.

If the dog continues growling despite your training attempts after four or five meals, and especially if your dog shows signs of aggression, such as growling or snapping other than at mealtime, enlist the help of a professional to handle the problem immediately. You'll want a pet behavior specialist who has experience working with aggressive dogs. Your veterinarian should be able to help you find someone qualified.

My breeder recommended home cooking for my puppy. Is this really necessary?

No, it isn't. There are many excellent commercial foods available today that provide all the nutrition your puppy needs. Most veterinarians would agree. However, if the breeder was feeding your puppy home-cooked food, you will want to do the same for the first week or so and gradually convert the dog to the food you choose to feed her, since any rapid switches in diet can upset a dog's digestive system. Get the recipe from the breeder.

Should you decide to continue cooking for your dog, be aware that you must learn how to prepare meals that have all the nutrients growing puppies need. Dogs are carnivores, and their diets should contain meat. They require adequate amounts of protein as well as other nutrients. Your breeder or veterinarian can provide guidance. You may want to give the puppy vitamins if you provide home-cooked meals.

If, like most dog owners, you decide to feed a commercial food, buy a name-brand product guaranteed to provide all the necessary nutritional requirements. At your local grocery store, just two of several name brands available are Pedigree and Purina. Both have formulations designed just for puppies. At pet stores and in many veterinary clinics you can buy premium dog food brands, such as Science Diet or Iams, which also have formulations designed to meet a puppy's nutritional needs.

Generally, dry dog food is more economical than canned, wet dog food. Many experienced dog owners and breeders believe that a diet primarily of dry food, mixed with a small amount of wet food to increase palatability, is a good choice.

Some owners and breeders have become concerned about the presence of preservatives and dyes in dog foods, which they believe are unhealthy. In response to these concerns, several dog food manufacturers now sell products that are dye-free, and an increasing number of dog foods are preserved naturally with vitamin E (tocopherol). If you want a product that is even more "natural," look in pet stores. Ask your veterinarian for a recommendation if you are uncertain about which brand to select.

Vitamins

Should you give your puppy vitamins? Opinions vary widely among the experts. Some believe that for healthy puppies on a good commercial diet, vitamins are a waste of money. Others believe that giving a vitamin supplement, especially antioxidant vitamins, such as vitamin E and beta-carotene, might help ward off diseases that develop later in life. This is a decision you'll have to make for yourself.

If you want to give your pet vitamins, be sure to have your veterinarian check out the product you want to use. Also, be sure to give the vitamins in recommended amounts, because some vitamins can be toxic if given in high doses.

My puppy is more finicky than my cat. She's rejected dry food and some canned food.

Most dogs will eat just about anything you give them, but some are finicky. In my experience, small dogs are more likely to be picky eaters than large dogs, although this could be because small dogs more often are "lap" dogs, and their owners fuss over them more. First, make sure you are not expecting your puppy to eat a total quantity of food daily that is more than she needs for her size. (I've found that the daily recommended amount on commercial dog foods is often more than many dogs need.) And do not give her any between-meal snacks.

Then, make sure the dog is hungry when you offer food. If you've been feeding three times a day, and she is over six months of age, cut back to two meals. Unless your veterinarian recommends otherwise, serve the same amount of food you've been giving daily, but give it in two instead of three meals.

The other way to make sure the dog is hungry is to delay feeding time; if you have been giving her the first meal at 8 A.M., wait until noon. (Remember, no treats.) This may be enough to cure the problem.

If not, try to identify one brand of good-quality food she seems to like more than others. Stick to that brand. Give her one "flavor" at one meal and another "flavor" at the next — for instance, canned chicken for one meal and canned beef for the next.

After you put the food down, do not coax her to eat. Do try and provide a quiet environment for the dog's meal, since some young dogs can easily become distracted from eating. If she doesn't eat the food after it sits there for about 20 minutes, pick it up, say nothing, and put it away. Don't feed her again until her next planned mealtime.

You don't want to do anything punishing, but you do want to get the point across that if she doesn't eat when you give her food, she doesn't get any attention. When you open one can of food after another and set each before her in your attempt to please her, she's getting lots of attention from you.

If she has no signs of distress with this feeding method, such as a loose stool, and if she's eating enough to maintain adequate weight, continue this strategy. Switching flavors among one brand of wet food shouldn't upset her tummy, as might a rapid switch from dry to wet food.

To keep from wasting costly pet food, cover and refrigerate uneaten portions. Give her a new can and another "flavor" for the next meal, but reuse the refrigerated food within the next day or two. She may find cold food unpalatable, so take the chill off in the microwave or by letting the food come to room temperature for five to ten minutes.

If your dog continues to completely refuse all food for more than two or three days, or if she is eating the recommended amounts of food but is losing weight, consult your veterinarian right away to make sure there isn't a medical explanation for her finicky behavior.

Once she is eating her wet food, start trying to gradually mix in some dry, crunchy food. By gradual, I mean just a few morsels of dry food initially. Increase the amount of dry food by just a few morsels daily. Dry food will help keep her teeth clean and produce a firmer stool, which is easier to clean up.

If she refuses the dry food and eats around it, try this: Put some dry food in a bowl, and add just enough water to cover it. Then microwave the food just enough so it starts to absorb the water. Let the food sit, absorb the rest of the water, and cool. Then smash it up, and mix with the wet food. Gradually increase the amount of dry food. Once the dog becomes accustomed to the taste of the dry food in her meal, you might be able to add it without softening it first.

Our puppy is healthy but overweight. She gobbles her food and begs constantly for more.

You can tell a puppy is getting too fat when you can't feel the ribs easily, and the dog's natural shape starts to become obscured. If that's the case, it is definitely time to cut down on the amount of calories the dog is getting and increase her exercise.

Keep in mind that puppies need more nutrients than older dogs because they are growing, so make sure you continue to feed her a product guaranteed to provide a balanced diet for puppies; do not switch to a "Lite" food, which is generally intended for adult dogs.

Next, check with your veterinarian to see how much of her food she needs to consume for adequate nutrition. Then try supplementing it with a food that has few calories, such as rice or canned green beans, which will help fill her up.

Also watch the treats. Often, it's the between-meal snacks that are responsible for dogs being overweight. Reserve a portion of her regular food to use for snacks or for the treats you may use for training her. Or, only give her very low-calorie snacks. Some dogs love bits of vegetables, such as carrot pieces, or an apple slice. (Introduce these very gradually, since they could cause gas.)

How can I get our pup to stop eating the cat's food?

You probably can't! It's just too tempting. In fact, it is unrealistic to expect a puppy or dog of any age to stay away from the cat's food. An owner who is really dedicated to obedience training probably could train a dog to stay put while the cat is eating; but for most owners, I think it's easier to simply separate the cat from the dog at feeding time. Either feed them in separate rooms, or feed the cat up on a counter out of the puppy's reach. I put up a baby gate to separate my dog from the cats while they eat.

When our puppy eats, he puts the food on the floor and eats from there. It's a mess!

Chances are your puppy is eating canned, wet food that has big chunks of meat. Try cutting up the chunks into smaller pieces before serving.

Or, try changing bowls. Make sure the one you select is large enough for the dog to eat from comfortably and that it isn't too deep. Some dogs don't like eating out of a stainless steel bowl but will eat out of a ceramic bowl (or vice versa). My dog won't eat out of a deep, stainless steel bowl with sides that are perpendicular to the floor, but he will eat out of a stainless steel mixing bowl, which has sloping sides. Some puppies do better with a nearly flat plate.

If you are sure the bowl is not the problem, say "No" as soon as the dog puts the food on the floor, then pick up the food and put it back into the bowl before he has a chance to eat it off the floor. Praise the dog for eating out of the bowl. Keep doing this until the dog gets the message.

To reduce the mess on the floor, spread out a section of newspaper under the bowl, then toss the paper after the dog eats.

Food and Water Bowls

Buy sturdy bowls for food and water that cannot be overturned easily or break easily and leave sharp pieces that could injure your puppy. Stainless steel bowls are a good choice, unless you have a puppy that doesn't like to eat out of this kind of bowl. Avoid plastic bowls, and watch out for bowls with parts that come off. I once bought an attractive dog bowl made of molded plastic, only to find that it had little plastic "feet" to keep it from slipping. The puppy readily chewed them off, and they easily could have presented a choking hazard had I not caught him in the act.

If you have a large-breed dog that will grow to be tall, consider purchasing bowls that are elevated in a stand. Some of these are adjustable. Elevated bowls can make it easier for large dogs to eat and prevent them from "splaying" their legs during mealtime. You can use the bowls on the floor until the dog is tall enough to warrant using the stand.

Our puppy plays in his food bowl. How do we get him to stop?

This behavior often stops as puppies get older. In the meantime, check pet catalogs for bowls especially designed for puppies. They are made of stainless steel but are raised in the middle, making it a little more diffi-cult for puppies to play in their bowls and making it easier for the puppy to eat the food.

If possible, avoid giving the puppy the opportunity to play in his bowl by removing it right after he eats. If he starts playing in his bowl before he even starts to eat, issue a "No no," remove the bowl, wait several min-utes, and put it back. Repeat the "No no" and remove the bowl again. Eventually, he'll get the message that he shouldn't play in his bowl.

This may not be a feasible solution if the puppy is alone in his "space" and you are leaving food out so he can "free feed," which is a common method of feeding puppies under six months of age. If this is the case, there is virtually nothing you can do to stop the behavior. You'll have to hope he outgrows it, and work on teaching him not to play in his bowl when you are home.

Our puppy plays in his water bowl and splashes the water out all over the floor. Can I stop him?

Use a very heavy water bowl, then set it on a mat, layers of newspaper, or a thick towel (without strings or fringe that he might be tempted to eat) so it's easy to clean up if he does splash. If you are going out, don't put too much water in the bowl. Add the amount you think he'll need to quench his thirst, but not enough to tempt him to play in the bowl. Be sure to replenish it often, because adequate water is vital to a puppy's health.

When he starts splashing around in your presence, scold him with a sharp "No!" Pick up the bowl immediately, put it on the counter, and stop interacting with the dog — do something else for several minutes. Set down the bowl again casually. If the puppy goes after it again, scold again and pick up the bowl, waiting even a few minutes more this time before setting it down again. The dog will learn to associate splashing with no water bowl and no attention. Like playing in the food bowl, puppies usually outgrow this kind of mischief.

My dog eventually stopped playing in his water bowl, but in the process of splashing around he learned that he can use the bowl to cool off. Now, after we have a play session on a warm day, I often find him standing with both front feet in his water bowl! He may get a little water on the floor when he takes out his paws, but I do not consider this an "offense" worth scolding. I think it's rather clever.

Our puppy sometimes vomits right after eating. Does this mean she's sick?

Eating too fast and too much, especially followed by playing after eating, often causes vomitting. Try feeding her smaller portions more often, and/or keep her from jumping around for an hour or so after feeding time.

If activity after eating is not the problem, she might have a food intolerance, which occurs in some dogs. Try changing the type and brand of food you are using, but do it gradually over the course of several days.

If the problem continues despite these efforts, or if the dog starts to vomit at times not associated with mealtime, vomits repeatedly, or throws up blood, check with your veterinarian right away.

Our puppy eats grass. Is this normal? Will it hurt her?

This is very common behavior, although no one knows for sure why some dogs like to eat grass. Some people believe it means the dog has an upset stomach and eats grass to induce vomiting, but plenty of dogs without tummy upsets eat grass. Other people believe that eating grass signals some kind of nutritional deficiency. In fact, some companies now sell products that are supposed to provide nutrients they say the puppies must need if they are eating grass.

Eating excessive amounts of grass might be cause for concern. In this case, I'd check with your veterinarian. If your dog is healthy and occasionally takes small bites of grass that has not been treated with chemicals, there is usually no need to worry. However, grass often goes through the digestive system just the way it went in, and then gets "stuck" in the rectum when the dog defecates. It has to be pulled out, and this can be an awkward mess if it happens when you are out walking the dog and you don't have a tissue handy. If you don't want your dog eating grass, try to distract her and get her moving on when she starts munching.

It is very important to prevent your dog from eating grass that has been treated with lawn chemicals, because some of them are highly toxic to dogs.

Avoid Chemically Treated Lawns

Don't let your puppy walk on grass that has been treated, because she could get the chemicals on her paws and lick them off later. Some herbicides, for instance, can cause severe gastrointestinal illness in dogs; some cause kidney damage and, in some animals, can even cause paralysis if the level of exposure is high enough.

Play it safe. Do not let your puppy onto a lawn treated with herbicides, pesticides, or fertilizers for 24 hours after the chemicals dry. If a granular product has been used, wet it down and don't let the dog onto the grass for 24 hours after it dries. You may have to wait for a good rain if you walk on grass that is community property or that is not in your own yard. If your puppy accidently treads on a treated lawn, wash her paws with a mild soap and water as soon as you bring her into the house.

Could it be normal for a puppy to eat her own and other dogs' feces?

Believe it or not, it is not unusual. This behavior has a name: *coprophagia*. We average owners call it just plain disgusting. It seldom signals a medical problem, although in some cases it can be linked to an inadequate diet.

Eating feces from other dogs is a potential hazard, because these stools might contain worms or be the source of serious infectious diseases, so be sure to keep her away from any piles of poop you find around the neighborhood! Eating her own stool is unlikely to make her sick, although it could upset her stomach.

There are several possible solutions. First, make sure she is receiving good-quality dog food. Most well-known, commercial name-brand foods designed for puppies have all the nutrients most young dogs need. You can buy products to put into her food that are supposed to make the stool undesirable fare. Or, you can put something hot, such as Tabasco sauce, on stools to train her that stools are not good to eat; but I'd only use this approach as a last resort. I think it's mean.

The best and least expensive approach is to simply pick up stools immediately after she goes so she doesn't get the chance to eat them. If she's been paper trained and is defecating and eating stools while you are not home (which you can tell by the smudge left on the newspaper), try to adjust her feeding and walking schedule so she defecates outside or when you are there to clean it up immediately. Make sure she has plenty of safe toys and chews to keep her busy while you are out, so she will be less likely to eat stool if she does go in your absence.

Puppies usually outgrow this behavior. If it persists, ask your veterinarian if the dog needs to be checked for some kind of deficiency.

Is there a way to keep our puppy out of the cat's pan?

Just as some puppies eat their own stools, some are attracted to cat feces, no matter how much you scold them. Most dogs love horse stools, too! Although puppies usually outgrow the tendency to eat their own stools, those that favor cat stools often continue this disgusting behavior whenever they have the chance. If they also ingest kitty litter, they are very likely to throw up the entire mess.

The best method of dealing with the problem is to make sure they don't get the opportunity, so put the cat's pan somewhere that is inaccessible to the dog.

If you have a large dog, wedge a pressure-mounted baby gate into the doorway of the room where the litter pan is located, leaving enough space at the bottom to enable the cat to crawl underneath, but small enough to keep the dog out. Or, block open the door just enough for the cat to get in but not the dog.

One pet owner I know had an opening cut into the bottom of a large closet in her basement. She even had it framed off with molding so it looks nice and neat. This closet is where she keeps the cat pans. The opening lets the cats in but keeps her dog out.

If you have a very small breed dog, keeping your puppy away from the cat pan is more difficult because he probably can go just about anywhere the cat can go. You may have to block off part of the house completely and keep the cat in the section forbidden to the dog. Or, put up a baby gate to block the dog from the room where you keep the cat pan; if your cat is young and agile, she may not mind having to jump over the gate.

This is definitely a problem that requires some imaginative thinking and resourcefulness!

To keep a puppy away from the cat's litter pan and feces, find a way to give the cat access to the pan, but not the puppy.

chapter **⑤**

Puppy Health
Concerns

our puppy deserves to be well taken care of. She will need periodic vaccinations by a good veterinarian; routine worming; spaying (or neutering if your pup is a male) unless you plan to breed her; and regular checks by you to keep her free of fleas and ticks. All these safeguards will keep her healthy and enhance your enjoyment of each other.

How do we find a good veterinarian for our puppy?

Ask several other dog owners in your neighborhood who seem knowledgeable to recommend a veterinarian. If you don't know any to ask, call several grooming parlors and pet shops, or ask a person on staff with your local humane society. Eventually, one or two names of veterinarians will keep coming up.

Keep in mind that pet owners often select the clinic that is the most convenient to their home. Convenience is important, especially if you ever have an emergency, but it should not be the only factor to consider.

When you ask people to recommend a veterinarian, find out why they like the one they are recommending. If they say, "The clinic's across the street from my house," they aren't offering very useful information. Encourage them to elaborate about experiences they've had at the clinic. You don't want to hear, for instance, as I once did, that a pet owner had an emergency, but when she called the clinic she had been patronizing for years, she was told the staff was too busy to see the pet. To me, that's unacceptable service.

In another case, a friend of mine took a pet to an older, semiretired veterinarian to inquire about having the animal spayed. The veterinarian was kind and friendly, but he had no staff and would have had to spay the animal by himself, without assistance. This indicates to me that the clinic is outdated, and I wonder if this veterinarian does enough surgical procedures to stay proficient.

Here is a short list of factors that I think make a clinic worth trying:

- **The clinic is clean.**

- **The clinic is well staffed.**

- **The staff is friendly and helpful.**

- **The clinic operates efficiently.** For instance, it routinely sends out reminders for vaccinations and any other care that dogs require periodically.

- **The clinic responds promptly** and with concern to owners' inquiries.

- **The clinic seems to have up-to-date equipment.**

- **The clinic staff is interested** in educating owners about their pets' health care.

- **The staff treats animals with compassion.**

Once you get the name of a veterinarian you think you want to try, call and ask the receptionist a few questions, such as whether they take new patients or what their hours of operation are. Calling the office will give you an idea if the staff is cooperative and friendly.

If you are very concerned about cost, do not hesitate to ask about prices for various services. There are many fine veterinarians around; invest some time in finding one.

Are vaccinations really necessary? They're quite expensive.

When many puppies come to their owners, usually around two months of age, they have often had their first series of shots. At least two more series of injections generally are required, depending on the vaccine products your veterinarian uses. After puppyhood, most dogs only need to be vaccinated annually.

The diseases that routine vaccinations prevent, such as rabies, are deadly. Some of them, such as distemper and parvovirus infections, have an affinity for puppies. Even if a dog survives a serious infectious disease, such as leptospirosis, he could be left with secondary problems, such as chronic kidney disease.

If you ever doubt the need for vaccinations, consider the symptoms for some of the diseases they prevent. Distemper causes a high fever, diarrhea, and jerking-like movements or seizures. There is no specific treatment, which makes preventing this disease the only logical course of action.

Many other infectious diseases that can affect dogs are similar: They cause horrible illness, there is no specific treatment once they occur, but they can be prevented in most dogs through vaccination.

By having your dog vaccinated routinely, you also are preventing the spread of infectious disease throughout the dog population in general. Keep in mind, too, that rabies vaccination is required by law in most states, because rabies can be contracted by humans.

Some veterinarians who specialize in homeopathic medicine question the need for some of the vaccines routinely given to puppies. However, the large majority of mainstream veterinarians strongly believe that the best way to keep dogs free of serious infectious diseases is through vaccination. Like millions of other pets, mine have always received all the recommended routine vaccinations, and they

Emergencies

Once you find a veterinary clinic to provide routine care for your puppy, ask how emergencies are handled. Some clinics handle most emergencies themselves; others require that when they are closed, clients go to a local emergency clinic.

If you are advised to use an emergency clinic, call to learn where it is and keep the number handy near your phone. In this way, you will be prepared if you ever have an emergency with your puppy.

Diseases Puppies Are Commonly Vaccinated Against

Disease	Comments
Adenovirus type 2	Causes respiratory illness
Coronavirus	Causes gastrointestinal illness
Distemper	Occurs primarily in puppies and affects the nervous and respiratory systems, among others
Hepatitis	Primarily affects the liver
Leptospirosis	Primarily affects the kidneys
Parainfluenza infection	Affects the respiratory system
Parvovirus infection	Attacks throughout the body, including the gastrointestinal system and the heart
Rabies	Attacks the nervous system

There are other vaccines your veterinarian may recommend based on your puppy's risk for certain diseases. If you live in an area where Lyme disease is endemic, a Lyme vaccine might be advised. If your puppy will be staying in a kennel while you are out of town, your veterinarian may recommend a vaccine to protect against *Bordetella,* commonly known as "kennel cough."

Be aware that puppies will require a series of immunizations for many of the vaccines they initially receive, such as the distemper vaccine. Subsequently, an annual booster is usually all that is needed. Your local veterinarian is the best one to advise you about the vaccines your puppy will need and when.

have never contracted a serious infectious illness. So far, they have all lived out their expected life span or beyond. I know of dogs not so vaccinated that contracted serious diseases and died a miserable death.

Veterinarians do mark up the price of vaccines. But that's one of the ways they earn their living. When you take your puppy in for vaccinations, that's also the time most veterinarians give the puppy a very necessary once-over. For many dogs, the annual visit is the only time they see a veterinarian — because vaccinations help keep them healthy, many dogs don't need to go to the clinic more than once or twice a year after puppyhood.

These annual visits serve another purpose: They help you establish a relationship with your veterinarian and the staff at the clinic. This becomes very important if you ever have an emergency, and especially as your dog ages. You are more likely to receive personalized, attentive care from a veterinarian if you are a regular client, just as people are more likely to receive more personalized care from a physician who knows them. And veterinarians who are able to get to know their patients and clients can administer better, more comprehensive care. Consider the cost of vaccinating puppies well worth the price.

Wouldn't it be cheaper to give the vaccines ourselves in the future?

Vaccines ordered from a catalog will cost you less than taking your puppy to a veterinary clinic, but consider the following: Vaccines require very careful handling to be effective. They cannot be exposed to extreme temperatures. Once received, many of them must be refrigerated; but to avoid causing your pet discomfort, they must then be brought to room temperature before they are administered.

Some vaccines also require special preparation, or mixing with a diluent, before administration. And, of course, the injection itself must be given correctly; it may be intramuscular (into a muscle) or subcutaneous (into the skin). Veterinarian Jane Fishman-Leon says that several problems can occur when dog owners vaccinate their pets themselves. It's not that difficult to accidently inject the vaccine into the intradermal, or deeper, layers of the skin, which can cause serious swelling; or to hit the sciatic nerve, which can result in lameness. It's also possible to hit a vein. Furthermore, she says, some dogs may experience a reaction to a vaccine that can be life threatening and require immediate medical treatment, which most owners would not be prepared to administer.

Some pet catalogs that sell vaccines advise clients to have vaccines delivered by overnight or second-day air delivery to ensure the products are not exposed to very high or low temperatures. Special delivery costs about $8 to $15 and will eat up a good portion of the savings you were trying to achieve by administering the vaccines yourself.

Depending on where you live, you may or may not have problems obtaining the syringes with needles that are required to administer vaccines. One pet catalog that sells vaccines points out that in New York, residents cannot obtain syringes and needles unless they submit a "Certificate of Need" from the Bureau of Controlled Substances. Several states altogether forbid average residents from buying either syringes or needles. Laws in more than 20 states require rabies vaccinations to be given by licensed veterinarians.

Worming

Puppies need to be "wormed" routinely, but it's easy. Your veterinarian can prescribe a pill that only has to be administered once monthly. It will protect your dog against heartworm (a disease transmitted by mosquito bites) as well as the intestinal parasites hookworms and roundworms. Some of these products also protect against whipworms, yet another type of intestinal parasite. Worms are contracted in various ways — contaminated soil is a common source. Dogs can contract tapeworms by eating fleas.

Besides routine worming, your veterinarian is likely to advise a blood test for heartworm antigen once yearly to ensure your dog has not been exposed. Also plan on taking in a sample of your puppy's stool for testing at the time of his annual checkup. These measures all help ensure your puppy remains worm-free.

As you can see, giving vaccinations yourself isn't necessarily a simple or inexpensive endeavor, and you've got to know what you're doing to ensure they are going to be effective.

I'd say that if you are a breeder with multiple dogs to vaccinate, you could consider giving vaccines yourself if the laws in your state allow you to do so and if you can and will comply with proper vaccination procedures. You must be willing to seek training from your veterinarian or another expert on the handling and administration of vaccine products and any reactions that might occur. You'll also need to keep meticulous records for each animal you vaccinate to ensure your puppies receive all the vaccines they should. You'll still want a veterinarian to check your puppies' general health and provide vaccines you may be unable to administer, such as the rabies vaccine.

For any other dog owner, I strongly recommend relying on your veterinarian to see to it that your dog is properly vaccinated. If you are badly strapped for money and are worried about the cost of vaccinations, consider taking your puppy to one of the discount pet clinics offered by some national and local pet stores. Your local humane society may be able to help you locate them if they do not advertise in the local newspapers. In addition, many towns in New England routinely sponsor "pet vaccine day" with a local vet who comes to the town hall. The cost is far less than that of an office visit.

How do we administer pills to our puppy?

The easiest way is to mask the pill in a yummy treat. Most dogs love cream cheese. Give your puppy one small hunk first to make sure she likes it. Assuming she does, make a cream cheese ball with the pill in the middle. She'll probably gobble it down. Other soft cheeses, such as Monterey Jack, can be used, or you can put the pill between two small pieces of sliced cheese.

Even if the prescription says to give the medication on an empty stomach, this method of administration is appropriate, because a small amount of cheese does not constitute a full meal, says Dr. Mark Papich, a veterinary pharmacologist at North Carolina State University.

If it turns out you have a dog that eats the cheese and spits out the pill, you'll have to actually "pill" the dog. Try this method: Facing in the same direction as the dog, straddle her and hold her still with your legs. (If she's very small, get on your knees and straddle and hold her with

1. Straddle the puppy and open the top of the mouth with one hand.

2. Place the pill in the back of the throat with the other hand.

3. Hold the puppy's mouth closed while you stroke her neck to promote swallowing.

your legs.) With one hand, gently but firmly grasp her around the muzzle — behind both sides of her nose — and open the top of her mouth. With the other hand, place the pill far back into her throat, in the middle toward the back of her tongue. Immediately close the dog's mouth and hold it shut, and gently stroke her neck a few times to promote swallowing. Obviously, you don't want to hold her mouth shut for more than a few seconds, because the pressure on her nose will impair her breathing.

You can also buy a pill dispenser in pet stores or from pet catalogs for just a few dollars. It's a pen-shaped device you put the pill into, then administer. You'll still have to go through much of the same process described above to use this device, however.

Pilling a dog works best if you're quick about it. If you have problems, your veterinary clinic can provide you with hands-on instruction.

Is there an easy way to equally divide medication in tablet form?

Dividing pills evenly is important to ensure your puppy gets the correct dosage, says veterinary pharmacologist Dr. Papich. He suggests asking your local pharmacist to help. Pharmacists have equipment designed just for this purpose, and most will be happy to accommodate pet owners — we just don't think to ask them often enough.

You can divide the pills yourself with the help of a pill splitter, says Dr. Papich, which can be purchased at the drugstore, or with a one-sided razor blade — the kind used to scrape windows — which can be purchased at the hardware store.

Here's another possible solution: Ask the pharmacist before you fill your prescription whether a pill prescribed for your puppy comes in liquid form or a pediatric suspension. Many drugs prescribed for dogs are the same drugs prescribed for humans. Some, such as the antibiotic amoxicillin, come in a liquid

Health-Care Calendar

Designate a calendar to record puppy care. Use it to keep track of important preventive health care chores, such as monthly worming, flea prevention, and annual veterinary checkups. Keep it in a place you're likely to notice, such as on the refrigerator door.

solution for children, which can be easily administered to a puppy with a dropper or syringe. The pharmacist can tell you how much to administer based on your veterinarian's prescription.

Can we use common household painkillers, such as ibuprofen, instead of baby aspirin?

Absolutely not. Veterinary pharmacologist Mark Papich says, "I never recommend ibuprofen for dogs under any circumstances. The incidence of adverse effects, such as stomach ulcers, is too great, or a toxic overdose can occur." In fact, ibuprofen is now one of the leading causes of poisoning from over-the-counter drugs in dogs because it is so widely found in American households. The common painkiller naproxen is sometimes used in dogs, but it also can result in problems and should only be given as prescribed by your veterinarian.

Although aspirin is sometimes prescribed for dogs to relieve pain and inflammation, your veterinarian will have to calculate the correct dosage. Dogs with certain medical conditions, such as kidney disease, require less than the usual amount given to avoid toxicity. Overdoses of aspirin can result in a long list of problems including vomiting, respiratory problems, and even death.

"Remember," says Dr. Papich, "that even though dogs receive the same kinds of medication we do, such as aspirin, the doses intended for

Medications

Dr. Mark Papich, a veterinary pharmacologist, cautions dog owners not to give dogs anything in the medicine cabinet that hasn't been prescribed by a veterinarian, including antibiotics.

Tetracycline administered to dogs under one year of age, for instance, can cause their teeth to turn yellow and become brittle. Fluoroquinolone antibiotics, such as enrofloxacin and ciprofloxacin, have been associated with abnormal changes in joint cartilage when given to puppies, especially those under 28 weeks of age. "This means these drugs might impair joint development," Dr. Papich says. There are so many drugs available today that average owners can't possibly keep track of all the potential hazards that each may pose to puppies, Dr. Papich adds.

people are far higher than what dogs — especially puppies — can tolerate. The most vulnerable are young puppies under about six weeks of age; physiologically, they cannot metabolize and excrete drugs the way older dogs can. Very special care is required if they must be medicated."

Keep these painkillers and other medications up and out of reach from your dog. Puppies especially are at risk for poisoning, says Dr. Papich, because they are teething and tend to chew whatever they can find.

We found ticks on our puppy. What's the best way to remove them?

Grab the tick with a tissue or with a pair of tweezers, or put on a pair of latex gloves, and gently pull it straight out. You may have to twist a little to remove this creepy creature if it's got a good hold. The head might remain in but will dry up and fall out. Treat the area with an antiseptic after removing the tick, and *don't forget to wash your hands.*

In the "old days" we used to burn ticks, paint them with nail polish, or dab alcohol on them, which was supposed to make them "back out." Today, experts say this could cause ticks to regurgitate germs into your pet's skin. That's why the simpler method above is recommended.

What's Lyme disease? Is it a risk to my puppy?

Lyme disease is a bacterial infection transmitted by ticks that causes an arthritis-like illness in humans and dogs. The disease is named after Lyme, Connecticut, where it was first discovered in the United States in the 1970s. The disease is often publicized in newspapers and has received considerable attention in veterinary journals.

Some veterinarians practicing alternative medicine believe that all the attention paid to Lyme disease is much ado about nothing. They point out that many dogs are exposed to the organism that causes Lyme disease and that many of them, if not most, never become ill. Veterinarians practicing in Lyme-endemic areas, however, often see dogs with debilitating illness they feel certain is a result of Lyme disease. They have no doubt that Lyme is a serious and growing threat to dogs and people.

Whether Lyme disease is a threat to your puppy depends on where you live or where you travel with your dog. Lyme disease is most prevalent in Connecticut, New York, New Jersey, Pennsylvania, Maryland, Minnesota, and Wisconsin. Over 90 percent of cases of Lyme disease in people occur in these states, although at least some cases have been reported in about 44 states, according to the Centers for Disease Control. Exactly how many dogs have been affected by Lyme disease is more difficult to determine, but it's safe to say that dogs living in the high-risk states or dogs traveling to those states have an increased risk of contracting the disease.

The ticks that spread Lyme disease in the northeastern and north central states are deer ticks; in the western United States they are western black-legged ticks. They are much smaller than the common "dog" tick most of us are used to seeing. They are so small, in fact, that they look like a freckle unless you examine them closely.

Dog ticks can also spread disease, however, so be vigilant about keeping any type of tick off your dog.

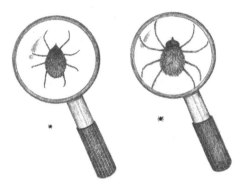

The deer tick (left) and the western black-legged tick that spread Lyme disease are much smaller than the common "dog" tick (right) that most of us are used to seeing.

Can I protect my puppy from contracting Lyme disease?

There are several ways you can reduce the likelihood that your puppy will contract Lyme disease:

Restricted access. Try to keep your puppy away from areas where ticks are likely to be found, such as tall weeds and thick woods.

Vaccination. Talk to your veterinarian about vaccinating your puppy against Lyme disease if you live in a state that's endemic for the disease. Veterinarians know better than anyone the risk for a dog contracting Lyme disease in their area, and there are now several vaccines on the market designed to prevent this disease.

Tick collars or repellent sprays. If your puppy will be going somewhere known to be infested with ticks, or will be routinely exposed to ticks, ask your veterinarian to recommend tick collars or repellent sprays that would be safe for use on your puppy. They will help minimize the tick population on the dog. There's also a new product on the market that kills both fleas and ticks (see the information on a product called Frontline that appears on page 79 with information on flea control).

Careful examination. Anytime your puppy might have been exposed to ticks — which may be daily in some cases — and whether or not he's been vaccinated and you have used tick repellant products, carefully examine him for the presence of ticks. Take extra care to look around the ears, which ticks seem to favor. Work your way systematically over every inch of the dog by running your hand against the hair coat to expose the skin. Go over the dog with a flea comb or shedding blade, which can help remove ticks you may not see with your eye. Rolling your dog's coat with a pet hair roller, which is basically a big roll of masking tape, might also remove any ticks still on the surface of your puppy's coat.

By preventing your puppy from exposure to tick bites, you can greatly reduce the chances that he will contract Lyme disease. Even when you find an imbedded tick that might transmit this infection, you can reduce the chances that your dog will become ill by removing the tick promptly. In other words, the longer an infected tick is on the dog, the greater are the chances it will transmit the disease.

> ### Product Safety
>
> Be aware that some products used on humans to repel ticks are toxic to pets, especially puppies, so only use products that are labeled safe for use on puppies. Never use several insecticides on your dog and in his environment at once, unless you check first with your veterinarian — you might overdose the dog. In addition, the development of new pest control products may eliminate or reduce the need for dipping and spraying your dog and treating your house with insecticides.

Unfortunately, some dogs will contract Lyme disease despite their owners' best efforts to keep ticks off. Know the signs of the disease so that you can seek prompt treatment, which usually involves a course of antibiotics. Early treatment increases the odds that your dog will recover and lessens the chance that he will develop a chronic problem, such as lifelong joint trouble. The signs of Lyme disease include:

- **Limping,** which can move from leg to leg

- **Trouble getting up and down**

- **Swollen or hot joints**

- **Fever, lethargy, or listlessness**

We have fleas. Help!

Fantastic strides have been made in flea control. In fact, there are several new products on the market that enable you to control fleas by treating your puppy once monthly and that may eliminate the need for treating the house, which can be a costly and messy endeavor. Which of the products you use will depend on your situation and your veterinarian's recommendation.

One of these once-a-month products is a pill called Program, for use in puppies age six weeks or older. When a female flea bites a dog that has been treated with Program, the flea ingests an agent that prevents it from producing viable flea eggs. The life cycle of the flea is stopped.

There are drawbacks. For Program to work well, all dogs and cats in the house should be treated. Program does not kill adult fleas, so you may still see some live fleas hopping around until the product takes hold, or if your dog picks up new fleas. If you can't stand the thought of waiting until the treatment puts an end to fleas in the house, you could treat your house at the same time you start your puppy on Program. This product must be administered with meals, which the manufacturer says is necessary to ensure absorption.

If your puppy only occasionally has fleas and is not frequently exposed to areas where he will pick up a new crop, Program could be a

A flea comb (left), which has narrow teeth, can help find fleas on your puppy but can also help you discover ticks before they attach. A shedding blade (right), usually a grooming tool, is another way to help find and remove ticks. You'll still need to examine your puppy's skin closely with your eyes to be sure ticks aren't present.

good choice. Remember that it may take a few weeks for the product to break the flea cycle. This product probably would not be a good choice for puppies with flea allergy dermatitis, a skin inflammation that occurs when dogs are allergic to the bite of fleas.

Another new monthly treatment product is Advantage, which kills adult fleas. It also can be used on puppies, but not until they are 16 weeks of age. It is a liquid. A few drops are applied between a dog's shoulders once monthly, and the product automatically spreads and distributes over the dog's coat. The manufacturer says it is odorless, kills 98 to 100 percent of existing fleas within 24 hours, and prevents reinfestation for up to one month. Fleas die before they have a chance to lay eggs, thereby breaking the flea life cycle.

The manufacturer of Advantage also says the product brings relief faster than "competing products" (meaning Program). Fleas don't have to bite the dog first, as they do with Program, for Advantage to be effective. This product would be a good choice if your dog is often exposed to fleas, or if you can't stand the sight of live fleas. Advantage also might be a good choice for puppies with flea allergy dermatitis, since it should kill at least some fleas before they have a chance to bite your dog. The manufacturer says the product does not penetrate the skin.

Yet another new monthly treatment is Frontline, which can be used on puppies eight weeks of age or older. The manufacturer says that the product kills more than 95 percent of fleas for up to three months and 90 percent of ticks for at least one month. Over 95 percent of fleas are dead within 2 hours, and 100 percent are dead within 24 hours of application; most ticks die before they can attach, and 100 percent are dead within 48 hours. When it first came on the market the product had to be sprayed on, which was a drawback because most pets do not like to be sprayed and some dogs won't stand for it at all; but the company subsequently developed Frontline TopSpot, which is applied just like the Advantage product.

All these products have been approved by the federal government, which required data demonstrating they were safe. I am aware of one or two owners who say their pets developed blisters or hair loss in the area where Advantage was applied; these problems may or may not be related to the product. I have also heard of a few dogs treated with this alcohol-based product that rubbed up against a painted surface and removed the paint. On the other hand, I know several veterinarians (including my own) who have been extremely pleased with the product and routinely recommend it.

These are all relatively new products, and it is possible that some pets will be hypersensitive to them. Certainly, it would be prudent to watch carefully for evidence of any ill effects whenever you administer a new product to your dog. Of course, the products must be used monthly during flea season throughout your dog's life.

> **Fleas**
>
> Fleas are more than just a nuisance. They are a health hazard. Because fleas feed on a dog's blood, a seriously infested puppy can develop severe, life-threatening anemia. Fleas also can give your puppy tapeworms.

Are there natural methods of controlling fleas?

There are natural methods of controlling fleas on dogs and in the house, but whether they work or not is controversial. Some pet owners swear by them, and others say they are worthless. You may have to try a few and decide for yourself. They certainly require more effort on your part than the newer, commercial remedies.

One of the oldest recommended natural methods is to add brewer's yeast to your pet's food. I have personally found this does not work, although I did not combine its use with other natural methods of flea control, nor did I treat the house at the same time. Adding garlic to the pet's food also has been recommended for years as a remedy for keeping fleas off dogs. Eucalyptus is supposed to be a natural flea repellant, and some people soak cotton balls in it and place them around the house. If fleas are already in the house, though, I've always wondered where they go if the dog isn't handy.

You can also purchase herbal flea collars, herbal powders, and similar products at natural food stores. Here's another remedy I recently heard about: Take a long, shallow pan, fill it with water, and add two Alka-Seltzer tablets. The fizzing is said to attract fleas to the pan, where they drown. But if you have 100 fleas in the pan, there probably are hundreds more in the house, not to mention flea eggs!

If you want to further investigate natural remedies for fleas and many other pet ailments, get a copy of *Dr. Pitcairn's Complete Guide to Natural Health for Dogs and Cats,* by Dr. Richard Pitcairn, D.V.M., Ph.D., and Susan Hubble Pitcairn. Dr. Pitcairn is highly respected by veterinarians practicing alternative medicine and is considered one of the founders of homeopathic veterinary medical care in the United States.

My puppy is scratching so much and so hard it's keeping me awake at night! What could it be?

If she is about six months of age or older, it could be flea allergy dermatitis, says Dr. James Jeffers, a veterinary dermatologist in Gaithersburg, Maryland. It takes about six months of exposure to develop an allergic reaction, and flea allergy dermatitis is perhaps the most common cause of itching and scratching in older puppies, he says.

Dogs with flea allergy dermatitis usually scratch around the tail area, since that's where fleas tend to congregate. However, it does not take many fleas or flea bites to set off flea allergy dermatitis in a sensitive dog, and you may not be able to find live fleas at all, Dr. Jeffers says.

Instead, look for another sign of flea infestation, which is flea "droppings." These are tiny dark specks. If they are present, you can generally pick them up by combing around the dog's tail with a flea comb, which has small, tightly spaced teeth. Place the droppings from the comb on a white tissue or paper towel and apply some water; if the specks are flea droppings, they will turn a reddish orange color. That's blood from your dog that fleas have ingested, then digested.

The remedy for flea allergy dermatitis is environmental control of fleas, Dr. Jeffers says. Try bathing your puppy with a flea shampoo that is labeled safe for puppies. "If this doesn't work, head for your veterinarian's office. Take advantage of the new products on the market," he says. (These products are described on pages 77–79.) If your pet has a really bad case, the veterinarian might want to prescribe medication to reduce inflammation and relieve itching.

If there are fleas in your home, you may want to buy a product to treat the house, but it may be unnecessary with these new products.

Are there other causes of itching and scratching in puppies?

Yes, says Dr. Jeffers. Scabies, or sarcoptic mange, is a skin disease that is not uncommon in puppies, especially if your pet came from a kennel or pet shop that maintains less-than-optimal conditions.

Scabies is caused by microscopic-sized mites, which lead to extremely intense itching. The mites often can be found in the ears and on the face, chest, or abdomen. Some dogs with mites develop patches of hair loss and crusting of the skin. Scabies is also a disease that humans can contract from their dogs, so you'll want to get it under control immediately. If you suspect your dog has scabies, says Dr. Jeffers, take her to your veterinarian immediately, where appropriate treatment can be prescribed.

Cheyletiella mange, commonly called "walking dandruff," is another type of mange. It mainly affects puppies but is very contagious. You could contract this disease, too, so if your puppy develops heavy dandruff, especially on the back and neck, run to the veterinarian's office!

A less common but possible cause of itching in puppies is food allergy. Dogs with this condition can itch and scratch anywhere on the body.

Occasionally, they may vomit an hour or two after eating. Your veterinarian can prescribe a special diet to help determine if food allergy is the culprit and help you find a diet the dog can tolerate.

Yet another cause of itching in puppies is inhalant allergies, Dr. Jeffers says. Dogs can become allergic to allergens they breathe in. The allergens that bother some dogs are often the same ones that bother allergic humans, such as dust mites or ragweed.

Whereas a dog with flea allergy dermatitis usually scratches around its tail, a dog with inhalant allergy is more likely to have an itchy face, which it will scratch or rub on the furniture or the rug. Dogs with inhalant allergies may also chronically lick their paws. Like flea allergy dermatitis, this type of allergy usually takes about six months to develop, so it's more likely to occur in older rather than younger puppies. Inhalant allergies are more common in some breeds of dogs than others, including Golden Retrievers, Cocker Spaniels, and terriers, but they can occur in any dog, Dr. Jeffers says.

Inhalant allergies can be treated symptomatically with antihistamines if they are not too severe; but if they persist over a long period of time, desensitization treatment may be in order. It will reduce symptoms in about 70 percent of cases, Dr. Jeffers says.

> **Reference Books**
>
> All puppy owners should have a good book or two on hand that provides basic information on first aid and health care. There are many wonderful books available at bookstores and in pet catalogs. My all-time favorite is *The Dog Owner's Home Veterinary Handbook,* by Delbert Carlson and James Giffin. I recommend that every dog owner purchase a copy. (See Appendix.)

Can we buy pet health insurance for our puppy?

You can, but companies selling pet health insurance are few and far between, and several have come and gone. There are a few prepaid health plans for pets modeled after HMOs (health maintenance organizations) for people, but they operate locally.

At this writing, the only company that sells pet health insurance in most states is Veterinary Pet Insurance (VPI) (see Appendix). It was founded in 1980 and currently has over 75,000 policyholders.

Linda Flores, a registered veterinary technician with VPI, explains how pet health insurance works. There are five levels of coverage. The most basic plan would cost about $50 a year for a puppy and generally covers up to $1,000 per incident per year, after you pay the deductible, or the first $40. The most expensive plan would cost about $160 annually for a puppy and would cover up to $4,000 per incident, after you pay the first $40. All plans have a benefit schedule, or maximum allowable amount for charges.

The cost of the premium would increase as your dog ages. For instance, it would cost about $60 annually to insure your two-year-old dog under the most basic plan. The annual premium would increase to about $80 when he reaches age five, and increase to nearly $110 annually when he is age ten. After age ten, the cost goes up annually.

The policy would cover the cost of caring for your pet if he is injured or develops a disease that is not excluded in the policy. If your Beagle develops allergies and the policy does not exclude allergies for Beagles, the policy would pay for allergy testing and would even pay for the cost of desensitization treatment, up to the limit of the policy, Ms. Flores explains.

Usually you would pay the veterinarian, then contact VPI to obtain reimbursement. A few veterinarians will wait to receive payment directly from VPI — most do not. However, VPI reimburses for claims within one week, she says.

What wouldn't this type of policy cover?

It would not pay for hereditary conditions, such as hip dysplasia; for preventive care, such as vaccinations; or for spaying or neutering. (The company is developing a special rider to its policies that would cover hereditary and congenital conditions.) Nor would it pay for conditions that could have been prevented through vaccination. For example, if you neglected to have your dog vaccinated against parvovirus, and your dog becomes ill with parvovirus infection, the policy would not cover the cost of treatment.

Unless the rider being developed would provide coverage, a VPI policy also would exclude some conditions that are common in certain breeds, such as atopic dermatitis (an allergic skin condition) in West

Highland White Terriers, cardiac defects in Boxers, and mitral valve defects (another kind of heart problem) in Great Danes. The same exclusions would apply to mixed-breed dogs: If your dog is half Great Dane, the policy would not cover treatment for mitral valve defects.

The VPI policy would not cover preexisting conditions, which are conditions that existed before you purchased the insurance. However, once a condition is "cured" and requires no treatment for six months, it would be covered — unless it is one of the conditions excluded for specific breeds.

In addition, the policy would not exclude a condition that developed once your dog is insured, Ms. Flores says. For example, say your dog got hit by a car and her leg was broken. Treatment would be covered, and if your dog had more problems related to this injury requiring more treatment the next year, the policy would cover that treatment as well.

Is pet health insurance worth the money?

Advocates of pet health insurance point out that advances in veterinary medicine, including the increasing use of high-tech equipment, have made pet health care more costly. It certainly would be nice to have pet insurance if your dog develops an illness or condition requiring treatment that would be covered.

Years ago, my Boxer developed a mast cell tumor. Tumors are a very common problem in Boxers, and VPI's policy excludes several types of tumors in this breed. It so happens that a VPI policy (if I'd had one) would not have excluded mast cell tumors; it would have paid for most of the expensive surgery that was necessary to remove this potentially life-threatening tumor. Unfortunately, there is no way to predict whether you will or will not need pet health insurance, or if your dog may develop an illness that will be covered by the policy. You probably are least likely to need pet insurance if you see to it that your dog receives routine preventive care and if you take measures to ensure your dog is never hit by a car or injured in some other way.

But then, insurance is all about insuring against the unexpected. It's a decision only you can make. If you would like more information about pet health insurance, you can find the address for VPI in the Appendix.

Should puppies be spayed or neutered, and are there any risks?

Spaying refers to removal of the female dog's reproductive organs, which include the ovaries and uterus. Male dogs are neutered, which involves removal of the testicles.

Some people used to believe that females should have one heat cycle before they were spayed, but this is now considered unnecessary and old-fashioned thinking. Females often can be spayed after six months of age. Males usually should be a bit older — closer to one year of age — before they are neutered; if they are neutered prematurely, or before puberty, it could interfere with bone development, especially in some of the very large breed dogs.

The most compelling reason to have your puppy spayed or neutered is to help keep down the population of dogs in the world. There are far more dogs than there are people to properly care for them. I think the only dogs that should not be spayed or neutered are those that are good for breeding because they have exceptional characteristics, such as good temperament and good health. And breeding should only be undertaken by people who know what they are doing or who have put a lot of time into learning about breeding.

Spaying definitely has benefits. It reduces the incidence of reproductive cancers in female dogs. It has the same effect in male dogs, although these types of cancers do not seem to be as common in males as in females. Spaying will spare you the chore of chasing away unwelcome male dogs that will come around the house when your female dog is in heat. It will spare you from having to clean up after a female dog in heat.

It is generally believed that spaying or neutering decreases the desire of dogs to roam; this certainly is true of neutered males, who will not be interested in seeking out females in heat.

The spaying or neutering procedures require general anesthesia, which always carries some risk. One primary concern is that the dog will aspirate, or inhale, stomach contents into the lungs and suffocate while under anesthesia. This risk can be largely eliminated by following your veterinarian's instructions to withhold food and water for about 12 hours before surgery.

How will I know when my female puppy is having her first heat?

Dogs that are in "heat," or the estrus cycle, may have swelling around the vulva and develop a discharge that initially is clear but then turns bloody. As the cycle progresses, the discharge may lighten in color. Your dog's behavior may be affected: She may raise her tail and act flirtatious around male dogs. But the signs of being in heat vary among individual dogs. In some, there are hardly any noticeable signs at all.

Females often have their first heat at around six months of age. If you will not be having your puppy spayed, be sure to protect her from an unwanted "puppy pregnancy" during the times she is in heat by preventing exposure to male dogs that have not been neutered!

What's the best method of taking a puppy's temperature?

You'll have to use a rectal thermometer. For about $16, you can buy a digital variety that can't break (as glass can) and that's very easy to read. These come with inexpensive but replaceable, thin, see-through covers that keep the thermometer sterile for each use. If you don't have one of these on hand and must use a glass thermometer, wipe it thoroughly with alcohol before use.

If you can, get someone to help. Have a helper firmly hold the dog to prevent him from sitting down.

Sweet-talk to the dog in a very pleasant voice and have some treats on hand to encourage cooperation. Smear some petroleum jelly (Vaseline) on the end of the thermometer and insert it about an inch. Now it's really necessary to keep talking to the dog pleasantly to distract him while you hold in the thermometer for about three minutes.

The normal temperature varies slightly among dogs, but it averages about 101°F.

Keeping
Puppy Safe

I t's terribly upsetting whenever a puppy wanders off and gets lost. It's heartbreaking when a puppy becomes injured or ill, especially from preventable causes, and it's truly tragic when a puppy dies because of owner carelessness. However, if you are trained with good information and you take certain basic safety measures, you can prevent these mishaps and ensure your puppy's well-being.

How can we prevent our puppy from ever becoming lost?

Make sure your puppy wears a collar and dog identification tag. Otherwise, the kindly stranger who may find her won't know how to get her home. Following are some other suggestions that can help prevent your puppy from becoming lost:

- **Training.** Train your puppy to "Sit" and "Stay" in the house when a door to the outside is opened (see chapter 11, Training Basics). Don't let her form the habit of running toward or out the door every time it opens. Until your puppy is trained, however, you must go out of your way to make sure she doesn't escape; even after she is trained, you still need to be careful.

- **Fencing.** This won't be feasible for everyone, but if you can, install a secure fence around your entire yard. If your puppy ever gets out of

the house when you don't want her
to, there's something to stop her.
Gates should be secure. Watch that
they cannot be left open by garbage
collectors, the mail carrier, or meter
readers. I have the gate in my back
yard locked so that it can't be opened
from the outside. (See also the dis-
cussion of underground electronic
fences in chapter 8.)

> ### Lost Dogs
>
> According to the National
> Dog Registry, one in every
> five dogs is lost or stolen each
> year, and most are never
> recovered. Millions end up in
> shelters, where they are euth-
> anized if not claimed. Others
> are sold by thieves for use in
> dog fighting, for cosmetic
> research, and even for food.

■ **Door locks.** If you have a household with young children running
in and out who might inadvertently let the dog out, you may want to
install door locks that cannot be opened by the children without
your assistance. Or, keep baby gates in hallways that lead to outside
doors to prevent the puppy from escaping.

■ **Company.** Be extra cautious when you have company. Visitors,
especially if they don't have a puppy themselves, just aren't aware
they need to be careful not to let the puppy out. When I have company in the house that's staying for a day or two, I keep a baby gate in
the hallway to the front door or lean a baby gate up against the door;
it reminds the guests not to let the dog out. If I have a group coming
over for dinner, I put the dog on a halter and leash and tie him by me
in the kitchen until everyone is settled at the dining room table.

■ **Repairmen.** If you live in an apartment, remember that repairmen
might come in and accidently let out the dog. Prevent this mishap by
informing your landlord that you have a puppy and ask that special
care be taken to ensure the dog doesn't get out. Anytime you know
someone will be coming in, try to be home. If you cannot be home,
put a note on the door that says, "Please do not let puppy out!" if
you're not worried about such a note attracting burglars. Then, put
the puppy in her "space," such as the kitchen with baby gates up.

■ **Leashes.** When you are walking your dog, always keep her on a leash. Make sure the collar, halter, and leash are all in good condition with no frayed spots or broken hardware. When you take your dog in the car, attach the leash to the collar before opening the car door to get out.

■ **Spaying or neutering.** Have your dog spayed or neutered; this helps curb a dog's desire to roam.

■ **Staying together.** To prevent your puppy from being stolen, never leave her unattended in the backyard, in the car, or by tying her to a post on the sidewalk while you run into a store.

■ **Record keeping.** Keep records that can help you locate your puppy if she's ever lost. For instance, keep a current photo that can be reproduced on posters, as well as a description of your dog (including any distinguishing marks, such as "white star on neck") and basic information such as her weight and height.

If our puppy becomes lost, what's the best way to go about finding him?

Here are tips from the Humane Society of the United States (HSUS), with some added comments from me:

■ **Contact animal agencies.** Telephone all humane societies, animal control agencies, and animal protection organizations within a 30-mile or larger radius of your home to file a lost dog report. I'd be sure to contact such organizations in all neighboring counties. I'd also physically go and walk through local shelters; I remember a case in which an owner was told over the phone there was no animal in a shelter fitting her dog's description, but when she went and looked herself, there he was! HSUS advises a shelter walk-through every 24 hours.

- **Search the neighborhood.** Walk and drive around and enlist the help of friends. HSUS says that early morning hours and sunset are prime times for finding lost pets. Also question neighbors, joggers, mail carriers, garbage collectors, and newspaper carriers; ask them to keep an eye out for your pet.

- **Use the power of scent.** Place a recently worn article of clothing in your yard. It might help lure your dog home.

- **Advertise.** Post fliers at places such as grocery stores, community centers, and churches.

- **Place an ad in the newspaper, and offer a reward.** (HSUS cautions that to deter potential scams, you should protect yourself by leaving out one of your dog's identifying characteristics to prove your pet has really been found.)

- **Notify local veterinary clinics.** If your dog was injured, he might have been taken for medical treatment before transfer to a shelter.

- **File a police report** if you suspect your puppy was stolen.

- **Use the Internet** if you have a computer. The Agriculture Department's Animal and Plant Inspection Service has created a Web site where people can advertise found and missing pets, including their photographs. The site is: www.aphis.usda.gov/reac.

HSUS also says that if your puppy is lost, don't give up hope. Animals that have been lost for months have sometimes been reunited with their owners.

Are there any special methods of identifying dogs or organizations that help recover lost pets?

Yes. There are several. The method I like the best is identifying a dog by tattooing it on the inside thigh with the owner's Social Security number and "NDR," which stands for the National Dog Registry. Your veterinarian can provide this service. NDR has been around since the 1960s and is dedicated to uniting lost pets with their owners. Many shelters and police departments know what it is; when they see the tattoo, they will know to contact the organization, which in turn will contact you. *Please don't make the mistake of having your dog tattooed and then failing to register it with the NDR!* (See the appendix for address and phone number.) Register your dog at the same time it is tattooed. If you don't register, and your puppy is lost then found, the organization won't be able to reunite the two of you.

Should you chose this method of protecting your dog, check with your local shelter to make sure it knows about the NDR. If it doesn't, ask the NDR to send information to your shelter.

The NDR says that for $38 you can register as many pets as you want. If you own a service dog, such as a Seeing Eye dog, there is no charge; and seniors age 62 and over get a 10 percent discount. If you're sure you only want to register one pet, the cost is only $15. The tattooing process, says the NDR, is painless, takes two minutes, and requires no anesthesia. Sally Fekety, director of sheltering issues at the HSUS, cautions that a dog should never be tattooed on the ear; thieves can simply cut it off, she sadly points out.

I like the tattooing method because it's a permanent form of identification that can't come off, as a collar and tag might. A tattoo on the inside of the leg also is obvious, and reputable medical labs will not buy a dog that is tattooed — something dog thieves well know. The tattoo consequently serves as a deterrent to dog theft.

Another option is to sign up with an organization such as the National Pet Protection Network (see Appendix). For a nominal charge, this company will give you a special identification tag for your dog; the tag has an 800 number to call and offers a $100 reward for whomever finds the dog and calls in. The network then contacts you so your pet can be returned. There are other organizations that operate similarly.

Yet another method is "microchipping." A small microchip with your dog's identification number is implanted, generally in the skin at the nape of the neck. A handheld scanner can "read" the microchip. More shelters today are buying scanners to check for microchips. However, Ms. Fekety of HSUS says that many shelters refrained from adopting the scanning systems because there was fragmentation in the industry. There are only a few companies that sell these systems, and each is different. If you lived in one place where the shelter used one system and you later move, the shelter in your new town might use another system and its scanner wouldn't be able to read your dog's microchip. The major players in the microchip industry recently resolved this problem by developing a universal scanner.

I see one downside to microchipping: A microchip is not readily visible and will therefore not serve as a deterrent to the theft of a dog, as a tattoo will. On the other hand, some veterinarians predict microchipping is the wave of the future and will vastly improve pet recovery as more dogs are "chipped" and more shelters use universal scanners.

How can I stop my puppy from eating all my houseplants and digging the dirt in the pots?

Keeping your puppy away from plants is important, because some plants are toxic or poisonous to dogs and can cause illnesses ranging from a mild rash to respiratory failure and death. When you have a puppy in the house, it is wise to remove plants unless you are absolutely certain they are safe for the dog. Alternatively, they must be put way up and out of the puppy's reach.

See the box on page 93 for a list of twelve common houseplants that are *unsafe* for dogs to eat and twelve common houseplants that are *generally considered safe* — assuming you haven't treated them with any toxic chemicals, and that there are no stones or pebbles in the pot that your puppy could eat. Pebbles covering dirt in pots can be ingested and cause an intestinal obstruction, which is a surgical emergency.

Once you are certain the plants in your house are safe for the puppy, then worry about training him to stay away. Certainly, tell the dog "No" if he persists in investigating the plants and simple distraction does not help. Buy Bitter

> ### Poison Control Center
>
> Ask your veterinarian to provide a phone number for a poison control center for pets. Keep it posted near the phone, and use it if your puppy ever ingests anything that might be poisonous and your veterinarian's office is closed.

Common Houseplants: Toxic or Safe?

Toxic	Safe
Aloe vera *(Liliaceae)*	African violet *(Saintpaulia)*
Boston ivy *(Parthenocissus tricuspidata)*	Bamboo palm *(Chrysalidscarpus lutescen)*
Caladium *(Araceae)*	Boston fern *(Nephrolepis exaltata)*
Dumbcane *(Dieffenbachia)*	Coleus *(Labiatae)*
English ivy *(Hedera helix)*	Grape ivy *(Cissus incisa)*
German ivy *(Senecio mikanioides)*	Hibiscus *(Malvaceae)*
India rubber plant *(Ficus elastica)*	Jade plant, Japanese rubber plant *(Crassula argentea)*
Mistletoe *(Phoradendron flavescens)*	Prayer plant *(Maranta leuconeura)*
Philodendron *(Araceae)*	Spider plant *(Chlorophytum commosum)*
Potted chrysanthemum *(Compositae)*	Swedish ivy *(Plectranthus oertendaklii)*
Weeping fig *(Ficus benjamina)*	Wandering Jew *(Tradescantia fluminensis)*
Yew (Taxus)	

Apple or another deterrent product. These are liquids or sprays that have a very unpleasant odor or taste. Saturate a piece of scrap material with whatever product you choose, and put the material under or around the pot of the plant. After the dog encounters this unpleasant odor several times, he should stay away. You'll need to respray the deterrent often — probably several times a day for the first few days until the dog gets the message.

I've heard there's a new kind of antifreeze that's not dangerous to dogs. Is this true?

Yes, this is true. Traditional antifreeze is another substance you want to be especially sure your puppy doesn't get into. It only takes about two ounces of antifreeze to kill a dog, and puppies are at even greater risk because of their small size. Symptoms of antifreeze ingestion are vomiting, staggering, then collapse. Antifreeze ingestion causes kidney failure.

A 1996 survey of veterinarians indicated that at least 118,000 dogs and cats had been poisoned by antifreeze during the previous year, and 77 percent, or 91,000, of the animals died. The study was sponsored by the American Society for the Prevention of Cruelty to Animals (ASPCA) and Safe Brands Corporation, a manufacturer. Antifreeze is estimated to account for about one in four accidental poisonings of dogs and cats, the ASPCA says.

The toxic element in traditional antifreeze is ethylene glycol. Unfortunately, antifreeze has a sweet taste that appeals to animals. Even when precautions are taken to keep it away from a puppy, there is always the risk of leakage or spills.

The new kind of antifreeze contains not ethylene glycol, but propylene glycol, which is safer. In fact, a food-grade version of propylene glycol is found in pet foods, cosmetics, and over-the-counter preparations.

One brand of this newer type of antifreeze is SIERRA. It was the first of its kind to be introduced to the market and is made by Safe Brands. A 50/50 mixture of SIERRA and water will protect a car's engine to -26°F; greater protection can be obtained by increasing the ratio of antifreeze to water, according to the company.

SIERRA is available nationwide. It costs about one dollar more per gallon than traditional antifreeze, but the price is little to pay if it eliminates a serious threat to your pets. See the Appendix for phone numbers to call for more information.

What precautions do we need to take to protect our puppy from hot weather?

Never exercise one of the short-nosed breeds of dog — such as the Pekingese, a Bulldog, a Pug, Boston Terrier, or Boxer — in hot weather. These dogs are prone to overheating and can collapse if you're not careful. They just don't breathe as efficiently as long-nosed dogs.

For other dogs, the risks aren't as great as they are with a short-nosed dog, but you still need to be careful. Dogs do not sweat as humans do and therefore cannot cool themselves as we do. Any dog subjected to prolonged exposure to heat or overexercise in very hot conditions could suffer heatstroke.

Hyperthermia and Hypothermia

Your dog is getting overheated (developing **hyperthermia**) and is at risk for heatstroke if his breathing becomes rapid and heavy. Overheated dogs often drool. Other signs of heatstroke include vomiting and, ultimately, collapse. If you think your dog is becoming overheated, soak him with cold water right away, including his head. If your dog seems near collapse, get him to a veterinarian's office immediately after soaking him down.

Your dog may be getting too cold (developing **hypothermia**) if he begins shivering. Remember that low body temperature can be life-threatening. Puppies as well as certain small and toy breeds can chill very easily. All breeds are susceptible to frostbite, too. If you think your dog is becoming too cold, bring him inside where it's warm and wrap him in a blanket. If he seems ill or near collapse, get him to a veterinarian's office immediately — keeping him well wrapped and traveling in a heated car.

Hot weather poses other risks. Dogs of any age can get sunburned, especially on their nose if it is light colored. Scorching hot pavement can burn their paws. They can become dehydrated.

In short, all dogs should be protected from hot weather. If the temperature is hot enough to make you uncomfortable, it's making your dog uncomfortable, too. In this kind of weather, only take your puppy outside for a walk or play session if you can keep him in a shaded area. Make sure he has plenty of water to drink, and if he still becomes warm, wet him down with the hose or a wet towel. For longer walks, wait until evening or early morning, when temperatures drop.

What precautions should be taken in cold weather?

Dogs can develop hypothermia — low body temperature — as a result of prolonged exposure to cold. In extreme cases, it can be life-threatening. Shivering is a sign that your dog is too cold. Puppies are more susceptible to cold weather because they are small. So are-small-breed dogs and dogs with short coats.

Dogs can also develop frostbite on their ears, nose, feet, and scrotum. In bitter cold weather — below freezing temperatures — great caution

must be taken with puppies. The
impact of cold will be even
greater if it's windy or raining
outside.

Some large-breed puppies
with a very heavy coat — such as
the Akita, the Saint Bernard, or
the Siberian Husky — certainly
can be taken for short, brisk walks
or an outdoor play session in very
cold weather, especially if the sun
is out. Moving around helps keep
them warm. But watch for signs
of shivering. If they shiver, bring
them in immediately. Even

A horse-style coat designed for dogs is
easy to put on and is a handy way to
keep your puppy warm on chilly days.

heavy-coated, older dogs that usually stay in a doghouse in the winter
should be brought in when the weather service issues frostbite warnings.

If you have a short-coated puppy, the temperatures don't have to
be freezing to cause hypothermia. These puppies may need to wear a

Coats and Sweaters

Many sweaters and coats manufactured for dogs are adorable, but not always
practical for male dogs. If the material underneath covers much more than
the chest and if it is loose at all, it may get soaked with urine, whether the
dog is hiking his leg or not. That's a mess for you, and it's uncomfortable for
a puppy to have on wet material in cold, damp weather.

An option is to buy your puppy a miniature horse coat — made for dogs.
They are available through pet catalogs. Addresses appear in the Appendix.
These types of coats cover the dog's back and attach with one wide Velcro
strip around the neck and another that goes under the chest. In very frigid
weather they will not keep the dog as warm as a sweater will, but they do
offer some protection, and some keep off rain quite well. They range in price,
but many of them cost about $30.

If you have a dog and find you need a coat but don't have one, try one
of your old sweatshirts or sweaters. If the waistband is too large, which could
cause the dog to trip, gather up the excess material over the dog's back and
tie it off with a heavy rubber band.

commercial doggie coat to stay warm if you have to take them outside for anything more than a short walk. Again, watch for shivering. Some small dogs should not be taken out at all in very cold weather. Boston Terriers, for instance, chill easily. Mine shivers when it's 60°F outside. So do many of the toy breeds, such as the toy Manchester Terrier, the Chihuahua, and the Affenpinscher. The Italian Greyhound also is prone to chills. With these dogs, you should put a coat on them before they go outside to do their "business." After they get the job done, they should come back inside immediately.

If your puppy becomes chilled, get him into a warm house and wrap him in a blanket. If the dog seems so cold that he appears ill or near collapse, take him wrapped and in a heated car to a veterinarian's office immediately.

What's the safest way to transport our puppy in the car?

The safest way is in a cage or crate secured in the backseat. This also would prevent him from jumping around. Don't forget, however, that care must be taken to prevent a dog from becoming overheated; never place a dog in a closed-in crate in a hot or even warm car!

Another method of transporting your dog is to buy a car seat for dogs that has a safety harness. These are suspended from the back of the seat and enable the dog to see out. However, car seats are generally only for very small dogs; some only hold animals up to about ten pounds.

You can buy a seat belt designed just for dogs; the strap goes over your dog's chest and then attaches to your car's seat belt. You could also teach your dog to lie down in the backseat, although I've found this can be difficult, simply because most dogs like to look out the window while traveling.

How do we train our puppy to ride in the car without jumping all over the place?

Car trips are an exciting event for many dogs, so expect your puppy to be excited. Perhaps the most important step in teaching your dog to behave in the car is to select a method you think will work with your dog, then stick to your car-ride training plan. Don't let him loose in the car during one trip, then expect him to use a doggie seat belt during the next.

If it's a car seat, for instance, put him in the seat, give him a treat and a pat on the head, and go for a short drive; and reward the dog if he's behaving well by sitting still in his seat. If he struggles to get out of his seat from the moment you put him in it, don't even go anywhere in the car the first several times; just put him in the seat, ask him to "Sit" and "Stay," and reward him. Once your dog starts to get the message that he's to be still in this contraption, take a short drive somewhere on a road without traffic where you can risk being distracted a bit. When your puppy tries to get out of the seat, put him back in immediately, ask him to "Stay," and tell him "Good boy!" Do it again and again. It will take several trips before your dog finally settles in. Eventually he will form the habit of sitting in his seat, secured by his halter and leash.

Air Bags

Beware if you have a car with air bags. There have been alarming reports of small children who were seriously injured or killed by the air bags, which can open with a force of about 200 miles per hour. Certainly, this could also seriously injure a dog, especially a small one. The risk can be reduced by moving the seat back from the dashboard; but if you have a car with a passenger-side air bag, it probably would be wise to train your puppy to ride in the backseat.

We want to take our puppy on a vacation, which requires an airplane trip. Is it safe to fly with a dog?

Unfortunately, there have been several reports in recent years about animals transported by airplane that were lost or that died. Dogs transported by plane usually have to travel in the cargo section, which is not temperature controlled like the passenger cabin, and can become quite cold or hot. I would not transport my dog by airplane, especially a puppy. Even if you book a short flight, takeoff and landing delays could leave your dog stuck in the cargo section for long periods of time while the

Car Safety

You've probably heard this warning, but it is extremely important and worth repeating: Never leave your dog in the car on a hot or even a warm day. The temperature in a car can soar to well over 100°F in just minutes, and your dog could become overheated and easily die, even if the windows are cracked.

I had a dog that became overheated even though the air conditioner was blasting because he was sitting in the passenger seat with hot sun beating through the window! Luckily, I had brought along a container of water for him and a bandana that I was able to soak and cover him with to get him cooled down. Then I moved him to a shadier spot in the car. I also know of a small, short-nosed breed dog that was placed in the back of a station wagon on a hot day in a crate that had solid sides and little ventilation; he was going just a few miles to visit the veterinarian but was dead by the time he got there. The dog got severely overheated.

Here are some other tips to help keep your dog safe when traveling in the car:

- On very warm or hot days, leave your puppy at home in a cool house rather than take him along in a hot car.
- For car trips that are more than an hour, especially in warm weather, take along a bowl and a plastic container of water for your dog.
- On long trips, stop every two or three hours to let your dog stretch his legs and relieve himself if necessary.
- Forbid your dog from sticking his head out the window of a moving car. He could get eye and ear injuries — or worse, fall out.
- If you need to open the window to provide air, only crack the window, or buy a device sold in pet catalogs (for about $10) that will enable you to open the window but block it with a grid that prevents the dog from falling out. Major pet catalogs are listed in the Appendix.
- The beds of pickup trucks on a hot day become scorching hot, which can burn the pads of a dog's feet. In some states, it is illegal to carry a dog loose in the back of a pickup. If you must transport a dog this way, invest in a special device that enables you to tie the dog in the pickup bed so he can't fall out, and only transport him when the sun isn't out and the temperature hot.

airplane sits on the runway or circles in the air. And if you want to take your puppy into another country, that country may have rules requiring your pet to be quarantined when it arrives.

If you must transport your puppy by airplane, consider these five recommendations, which were issued in 1996 by the American Veterinary Medical Association and the Air Transport Association:

1. Check with a veterinarian to be sure your pet is fit to travel. Most airlines require a certificate of good health signed by your veterinarian within the last 30 days. Your pet also will need a rabies vaccination certificate if the plane crosses state borders. He should wear a collar with an identification tag.

2. Pug-nosed breeds — such as Pekingese, Chows, Bulldogs, and Boston Terriers — often have trouble breathing at high altitudes and can become overheated easily. Airlines advise against transporting them by airplane.

3. If your puppy is very small — under about ten pounds — see if the airline will allow you to take the animal with you in the cabin. Your puppy must fit in a kennel that can be placed under the seat. (Service dogs, which assist people who are disabled, are generally allowed in the cabin even if they are large dogs.)

4. If your puppy cannot fly in the cabin with you and will be in the cargo section of the airplane, *book him on a direct, nonstop flight to minimize travel time. During hot summer months, avoid flights in the middle of the day. Instead, schedule an evening flight or one early in the morning when temperatures are lowest.*

5. Only give tranquilizers or sedatives to your pet before traveling if your veterinarian so advises; they can have adverse consequences at high altitudes.

These organizations also advise letting the airline know well in advance that you will be transporting your dog. Reconfirm flight times 24 to 48 hours before departure, especially during times when the weather is bad.

Pets must be transported in a portable kennel that meets requirements established by the U.S. Department of Agriculture (USDA). The kennel must be sturdy, well ventilated, and big enough for your pet to stand up, turn around, and lie down. It must be labeled with identification information and your pet's destination. The airline can provide more information. Pet catalogs sell crates that are approved by airlines; some cost around $100. If you take your dog in the airplane cabin with you, you'll probably need a ventilated nylon carrier designed for this purpose, also available in pet catalogs. These run about $50 to $60. In either case, check with the airline before investing in this kind of equipment to make sure that whatever you plan on getting meets their requirements.

The USDA also requires that dogs have food and water within four hours before the time of departure; you will be asked to sign a statement stating when food and water was last offered, and you will need to have empty water and food bowls in the kennel.

Is it true that chocolate is poisonous to puppies?

Yes. Chocolate is poisonous to dogs of all ages. Chocolate contains caffeine and theobromine, and dogs metabolize these substances differently than humans do. Giving a dog chocolate is comparable to feeding him several cups of strong coffee. It can result in vomiting, diarrhea, and "hyper" behavior. Serious cases of chocolate poisoning can even cause seizures and heart irregularities.

Baker's chocolate is stronger than milk chocolate; and the smaller the dog, the less chocolate it takes to cause a problem. In other words, if a tiny Yorkshire Terrier eats a square of Baker's chocolate, you are more likely to end up with a problem than if a German Shepherd dog eats a hunk of milk chocolate. Dogs and chocolate just don't mix, so don't let your puppy have any.

General Safety Tips

Make sure electrical cords are unplugged or inaccessible to your puppy. Dogs can electrocute themselves by chewing on them.

Be aware that Christmastime is especially hazardous for puppies. They can eat ornaments off the tree, pinecones and needles, or ribbon, which can all lead to serious intestinal problems. Keep your puppy out of the room with the Christmas tree unless you are there to supervise every minute. Also consider buying a smaller tree and putting it up on a table that the puppy can't reach.

Watch that your puppy doesn't get slammed in a door. It can happen more easily than you think if he's running in and out the back door with the kids.

Don't use continuous-cleaning toilet bowl cleaners. They will poison your dog if he drinks toilet water containing the chemicals found in these products.

Keep your puppy from strangling. Never, never tie a dog by its collar and leash to — or near — steps, a deck, or any other elevated place from which he could jump.

Practice fire-prevention techniques. Never leave your puppy in the house with the clothes dryer, dishwasher, or other appliances running. Never leave your puppy alone in the kitchen with the oven or stove on.

Never leave the lower sash of windows open, especially if you live above the ground floor. Even if you have secure window screens, dogs can go through them if they see something tempting outside. I know of two dogs — one a Cockapoo and one a Great Dane — that have both jumped out of second-story windows! Luckily, these two were not hurt, but it's a miracle they didn't break their legs.

Reluctant Pretty Puppy

Bathing, brushing, clipping toenails, cleaning teeth — you want your puppy to look and feel her best. But she may resist your efforts to keep her well groomed. If you introduce each grooming process gradually and reinforce it regularly throughout her life, she will adjust to and may even come to enjoy these opportunities to enhance her well-being.

Is there any way to get our puppy to like her bath? We get more water on us than on her.

Start by making her bath comfortable. Too often, owners get out the garden hose and soak the dog with ice-cold water, which is sure to make bathing an experience the dog does not want to repeat! If bathing is pleasant, dogs will love it. I've used the approach to bathing described below, and I've never had a dog that didn't like to be bathed. In fact, the dog I have now so likes bathing that he will leap right into the tub when I'm in it if I forget to close the door.

Before bathing your dog, brush her out well to remove loose hair and dirt. Use your bathtub for her bath or a large washtub where warm water is available. If you don't already have one, invest in a detachable showerhead with a long hose, or buy one of those rubber hose/spray combinations that can be easily attached and detached at the faucet.

Dogs are far more likely to accept a sprayer than immersion in water, and you'll get less water on yourself, too. Then:

1. **Put down a large, rubber, nonskid mat.** Most dogs will protest wildly if they are sliding around on a wet, slippery surface. Give their feet a good grip.

2. **Sit on the edge of the tub** with your feet inside the tub instead of kneeling over. This not only helps prevent the dog from jumping out, but it reduces the likelihood that you'll strain your back by bending over the tub. It also helps if you remember to close the bathroom door so the dog doesn't get the idea she can jump out of the tub and run out the door.

3. **Adjust the water temperature** so that it feels just barely warm on the inside of your wrist.

4. **Wet the dog's feet first** with the sprayer to get her used to the water. Talk her through this; use a very pleasant voice and say things like: "Isn't this fun! What a good girl!" Once you've got her accepting the water, go to the next step.

5. **Wet her neck** and work back down her body. (Forget washing her head for now.) You'll want to work from the neck back so that if there are any fleas hiding out, they do not escape onto her head.

6. **Lather her up next.** (You should still be talking pleasantly to the dog.) Then rinse, rinse, rinse! Every last bit of soap must be removed, otherwise it could irritate her skin.

7. **Use a washcloth** *without* soap to wash off her head and face. You don't want to risk getting soap in her eyes.

8. **Use your hands to squeegee** out as much water as possible. Help her safely get out of the tub onto a mat or towel on the bathroom floor, and rub her down with some thick towels. Some dogs can be trained to accept the blow-dryer, but be very careful not to burn the

skin. To prevent burning, keep your hand on the dog so you can feel part of the airflow and monitor the temperature, and move the dryer constantly.

Some dogs, especially those that have had unpleasant previous bathing experiences, must be introduced to bathing very gradually. This could mean that your initial goal will be to get the dog into the tub, without using water; then the next time or two, only turning on the water without wetting her. Once she accepts this much, then progress to wetting her feet before trying to move on to a full bath. Use praise and rewards all along. Make this an experience she wants to repeat.

When you are giving the dog a full bath, take pains to keep water out of her ears, because water in the ears can predispose to infection. To prevent this, many experts advise packing the dog's ears with cotton before bathing. If you are having trouble just bathing the dog, however, I would not pack the ears, at least not until the dog learns to welcome her bath. You don't want to do anything she associates with unpleasantness. But be sure to keep her head up when bathing by lifting her chin with one hand, and don't spray too close to the ears.

Okay, my puppy now accepts her bath. How often should I bathe her?

Veterinary dermatologist James Jeffers says that how often puppies are bathed may vary anywhere from once weekly to once every two or three months. It will depend on your dog's coat and lifestyle.

If you have a breed with a smooth, short coat — such as a Miniature Pinscher, a Boxer, or Toy Fox Terrier — and the dog primarily is a house pet that doesn't go outside and get dirty and doesn't get smelly, every few months usually is adequate. If your puppy has longer hair, a white coat that gets dirty easily, or goes outside and gets dirty often, more frequent bathing may be in order.

In short, bathe as needed, but avoid extremes. Bathing more than necessary can remove oils and dry out the skin; on the other hand, all dogs should be bathed at least two or three times a year to cleanse the skin and hair.

In between full baths, you can give your dog minibaths. Use a sponge or soft washcloth and wipe the face and head, around the tail, the feet, and anywhere else you think the dog might be dirty. Dry him well with a towel.

What kind of shampoo is best for bathing puppies?

For routine bathing, Dr. Jeffers recommends using a hypoallergenic shampoo designed for dogs. These shampoos contain only cleansing agents, and most shampoos designed for dogs have a pH (or acidity) that is compatible with a dog's skin. The pH in human shampoos really is different, he says.

Shampoos for dogs also are designed to rinse out easily, which is important. Dogs have a lot more hair than humans, so there is a lot more to shampoo and to rinse out. If a residue of shampoo is left on, it might irritate the dog's skin. In addition, a shampoo that rinses easily makes bathing easier; you cannot expect a puppy to be still as long as it might take to rinse out a very sudsy shampoo, Dr. Jeffers says. Only use special shampoos, such as a flea shampoo or a medicated shampoo, when you really need them; they can be drying to the skin if used often for routine bathing, he notes.

If your dog needs a bath and you don't have any dog shampoo on hand, a dishwashing detergent, such as Palmolive, Lux, Ivory, or Dove can be used in a pinch, or try baby shampoo. Mix some of the detergent with water — half and half will do — before applying it to the puppy so that it rinses out more easily. Do not use dishwashing detergents containing citrus, which can be drying to a dog's skin, Dr. Jeffers advises.

One word of caution: Some dogs with allergies will be sensitive to dishwashing detergents, to seemingly mild human shampoos, and even to some types of shampoos made for dogs. I once bathed my Boxer with baby shampoo and watched in horror as he rapidly broke out in huge hives over his entire body. It took a visit to the veterinarian and a week of corticosteroid medication before the hives went away. Besides hives, scratching after a bath may be a sign that the shampoo you used doesn't agree with your puppy's skin. In such cases you should contact your veterinary clinic, which can recommend a shampoo that is safe for use on your dog.

My puppy's eyes run, leaving stains on her face. How can I get rid of the discoloration?

The stain probably is caused by clear eye fluids that do not drain properly. In some dogs, ducts that usually drain eye fluid become clogged; in others, it's due to the dog's anatomy — the dog may lack ducts, or they may be malformed. The tears have nowhere to go but down the face. This is a common problem in small dogs, such as the toy Poodle and, sometimes, in larger dogs, such as the Cocker Spaniel.

Some breeders advise using a weak solution of hydrogen peroxide to remove the stains, but if it accidently gets into your puppy's eyes, it could cause discomfort and perhaps even injure the eyes. Opt instead for one of the commercial products made just for this purpose, which are labeled as nonstinging. A four-ounce bottle of these products only costs about $4 to $5.

In some dogs, blocked ducts that cause the eyes to run can be opened, but if your puppy is prone to this condition, it is likely to happen repeatedly. Ask your veterinarian. You'll also want to contact your veterinarian if the discharge from your dog's eyes ever becomes anything other than clear, which could indicate an infection.

My puppy's coat is dry and scaly. What should I do to eliminate this problem?

First make sure you are feeding your puppy one of the many name brand, commercial dog foods on the market. They are likely to have all the nutrients your puppy needs. Ask your veterinarian for a recommendation. Usually, feeding a good-quality food is all that is needed to maintain healthy skin and a glossy hair coat, says Dr. Jeffers.

Some breeds, such as Labrador Retrievers and Doberman Pinschers, tend to experience scaling in the winter, when the air in our homes becomes dry. You can usually eliminate this problem by upgrading to one of the "premium" dog foods advertised to promote healthy hair and skin, Dr. Jeffers says.

The quality of the name-brand, commercial dog foods on the market today usually eliminates the need to supplement your dog's food with eggs or oil to maintain a healthy, glossy coat; so unless you have a specific problem and supplementation is recommended by your veterinarian, save your money, Dr. Jeffers says.

Depending on their coats, dogs enjoy grooming with a bristle brush (left) or a rubber curry brush.

How often should I brush my puppy? What tools should I use?

Daily is ideal. Brushing removes dead hair, promotes circulation, and contributes to a glossy coat. It also keeps down the amount of shedded hair in your house. Few owners, however, have the time or inclination to brush daily.

Aim for at least two or three times a week if you have a dog with a coat that is simple to care for and doesn't require special care. Then step it up if this doesn't seem to be enough to keep your puppy's coat nice and neat. Dogs with very long coats — such as the Lhassa Apso, Maltese, or Afghan — probably will require more frequent brushing (often daily) to keep the coat looking its best.

If you have a puppy with a smooth, short coat — such as a Pug, a Beagle, or a toy Manchester Terrier — all you need is a grooming mitt. These fit over your hand, and you stroke the dog in the same direction the coat grows. A rough washcloth could also be used. My smooth, short-haired dog prefers a rubber "brush." This grooming tool has rubber "fingers" that massage the dog and also help remove dead hair and dirt.

There are many brushes designed for use on dogs with long coats. Some have soft wire pins. I would select one with balls on the tips, which helps reduce breakage of the hair. You might also want to invest in a good grooming comb, which should have rounded tips and adequate space between the teeth to easily pass through a dog's coat. For dogs with very heavy coats, buy a shedding blade, which helps remove dead hair.

If you have a dog with a coat that requires trimming, such as a Poodle, take your dog to a professional groomer or other expert, and have them do it or teach you how.

Dogs, such as Cocker Spaniels, may need the dead hair plucked out of their ears and from between the toes periodically. *Unless you have experience grooming dogs, have a professional groomer pluck out hair when needed or show you how.*

How can I get our puppy to sit still so I can brush her? She thinks it's a game and grabs the brush.

Start by grooming after a play or exercise session when the dog is tired. You'll have less resistance. Get down on the floor with the dog or put her on a table if she's small and you think she'll stay there. Then, hold treats in one hand and the grooming brush in the other. Ask her to "Sit, Stay," or tell her "Down" if she knows one of these commands (see chapter 11), then talk to her in a pleasant voice to provide a bit of a distraction; keep the brush low so it does not become the point of focus.

As soon as she's in the position you've asked for and is listening to your voice, run the brush down her back near the tail — the place furthest away from her mouth. If she goes after the brush, issue a moderately scolding "No No," and try again. The first time she stays still for a swipe of the brush, tell her "Good girl" and *immediately* give her a treat. Repeat, trying the brush on different parts of her body. Eventually, she'll learn this is a very pleasant experience and will become more cooperative.

Shedding

Although shedding can be influenced by factors such a illness or stress, it is primarily influenced by exposure to light. When the days grow longer in spring, dogs shed. Dogs that live indoors sometimes seem to shed constantly because they are continually exposed to artificial light. Of course, some dogs, like the Poodle, have hair coats that don't shed at all.

How do we get mats of hair out of our puppy's coat?

First, try separating as much of the hair as you can with your fingers. Then try brushing out the mat, starting at the end of the hair and working toward the skin. There are combs designed for dematting, but they can cause skin damage if not carefully used.

For some mats, it may be necessary to resort to using scissors. But be careful! Sandy Rippey, a professional groomer, says, "I've seen horrendous damage to the skin after owners used sharp instruments to cut out mats and cut toward the skin, or tried to cut parallel to the skin. It can be more difficult than you realize to tell where the mat stops and the skin begins." She strongly advises using blunt-ended scissors and holding them with the finger holes next to the skin and the end of the scissors pointing out — *perpendicular* to the skin. Put one half of the scissors through the mat and cut out, away from the skin, to break up the clump. If a dog has a lot of mats that are difficult to get out, it's best to have a professional groomer work on the dog, she says.

Mats between the toes should be handled in the same way: If they can be separated with the fingers and brushed or combed out with relative ease, owners can handle these mats themselves. However, if the mats are tightly wound around the toes, take the dog to a pro.

Ms. Rippey points out that in breeds with heavy coats and undercoats — such as the Keeshond or Newfoundland — proper brushing can go a long way toward preventing mats. Do not, she says, brush from head to tail and from the top of the back down the sides. Instead, start at the tail. With one hand, hold the hair back against the growth pattern, and with the other hand, brush it out a little at a time in the direction of the hair coat. Use the same technique to brush out the dog's underside, working up the sides, not down.

How do we get burrs out of our puppy's coat?

Pull the hair out of the burr, instead of trying to pull the burr out of the hair. Pull away just a few strands of hair at a time. Work on one side of the burr, then the other. It takes time and patience, but usually after you get most of the hair out of the burr, you can crumble the burr and remove it. You may even want to wear gloves, because burrs can stab your fingers.

How do I know if my puppy's toenails are too long? How often should they be clipped?

Dogs that are walked or play often on hard surfaces, such as concrete, may wear their nails down enough so that they rarely if ever need to be clipped. Most dogs that are indoors most of the time, especially on carpeted surfaces, routinely need their nails trimmed.

To tell if your dog's nails need to be clipped, have him stand on a hard, level surface, such as a linoleum floor. If the nails touch the floor, they are too long. Just how often you trim your dog's nails will depend on how rapidly your puppy's nails grow and how much they are worn down by hard surfaces. Some dogs require a nail clipping every couple of weeks; others can go for several weeks at a time without a clipping.

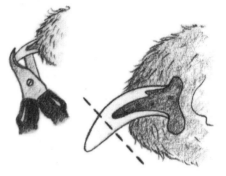

Identify the vein in your puppy's nail before clipping. Clip just below the vein.

It is best to trim a little bit from the nails often, rather than let the nails grow very long and try to trim off a lot of nail at once. Nails that grow too long can get caught on objects or hung up easily, which can result in painful injuries if the nail is torn from its bed.

How do I get my puppy to let me clip his nails?

Before clipping, play with his nails several times to get him used to the idea of your handling them. A good time is when the puppy is relaxed and dozing next to you. Also study the nail. Look for the place where the pink vein in the nail stops. Once he gets used to your handling his nails, prepare to start clipping.

Invest in a good pair of nail clippers. Old, dull clippers make the job difficult, and the puppy will be sure to resist. I prefer a European-made type of clippers that do *not* require a blade change. They are made of stainless steel, can be locked shut when not in use, and have handles that enable you to get a good grip. They cost about $12 and are available from major pet catalogs and in some pet stores and veterinary offices. Used only on one dog, one pair should last for years. I do not like nail clippers that require a blade change; I never seem to have new blades on hand when I need them, and I can never seem to get a new blade in correctly.

Once you have your clippers and are ready to clip, select a place where the light is good. I've found that bright, but indirect, sunlight is best. A bright lamp also may be adequate. Have treats on hand. Ask your puppy to lie down on his side, in a position that enables you to lift the paw and expose a nail in the light. With small dogs, it is sometimes easier to hold them in your lap. You'll have to experiment to find the best position for you. Use the "Stay" command (firmly if necessary), and then talk to your dog in a reassuring, cheerful manner. Clip the nail just *below* the vein. If your dog has black nails and you can't see the vein, take off only a very tiny bit at the end of the nail and hope for the best.

After a clip, immediately tell the puppy "Good boy!" and give him a treat. If he was still and accepted this clip well, continue. Do two or three nails this time before providing him with a reward. After a few sessions like this, your dog should learn to accept routine nail clippings, and it will take little time.

If the puppy was not cooperative, reward him after you've clipped one nail, then wait an hour or two (or even a day) before resuming clipping. You want the dog to learn that nail clipping is a positive experience. If clipping is forced on an unwilling dog and becomes unpleasant, you'll have a fight on your hands every time. Gradually work on your dog.

If your puppy's nails have gotten way out of hand and are far too long, do not cut them back to the desired length all at once! As the nail grows, so does the vein in the nail; conversely, as you clip a little from a nail, the vein recedes. Just clip off a little about once weekly until you get the nails to the desired length.

Even when you are careful, from time to time you'll probably nick a vein, which can bleed profusely. Apply direct pressure, or use a styptic pencil. The bleeding should stop in a few minutes. If *heavy* bleeding persists for longer than about five minutes despite direct pressure and use of a styptic pencil, call your veterinarian.

One other way to control nail growth is with an electric nail groomer, which grinds down the nail. These are available in pet catalogs and cost about $45 to $50. They make a very nice, neat nail and are popular among many breeders. The grinders, however, make a noise that many dogs don't like.

If you can't seem to get the dog to cooperate with nail clipping, enlist the help of your veterinary clinic or a professional groomer. The professionals can show you how to clip, or they will do the clipping for you if you aren't confident enough to do the job yourself.

Is it necessary to make cleaning a dog's teeth a routine part of grooming?

Keeping your dog's teeth clean is very important. Like people, dogs develop tartar buildup, which can lead to gum disease and tooth loss. Infections in the gum can spread to the sinuses. Gum disease can lead to other problems, too. Dr. Larry P. Tilley, a well-known veterinary cardiologist and author of the *Manual of Canine and Feline Cardiology,* says that gum disease has been linked to endocarditis — an inflammation of the lining inside the heart — in dogs with aortic stenosis, a narrowing of an important artery. Aortic stenosis is considered a relatively common congenital cardiac problem in certain breeds, such as Boxers and German Shepherd dogs.

Gum disease can occur in young dogs, although it is more common in older ones. Gum disease is more likely to occur if you live in an area with hard water, and if your dog eats mostly soft foods. The signs of gum disease include bad breath and bleeding from the gums when the dog chews.

You'll want to learn to clean your puppy's teeth not only to keep the teeth clean and prevent gum disease, but to get the dog used to this grooming chore. Most dogs will balk if their owners try to start cleaning their teeth when they are older.

How do I get my puppy to let me clean her teeth?

Start by playing with your dog's teeth. Do it after a vigorous play session when she is tired and you two are relaxing together. Just stroke her muzzle and then gradually start rubbing her teeth with your finger. Make it as pleasant as possible — like a mouth massage.

Once she accepts this much, add a piece of gauze to the regimen. (If your dog readily accepts having her teeth handled, you could try a small, soft toothbrush.) Wrap the gauze around your finger and rub her teeth. She'll probably be curious about the gauze and try to steal it at first, but encourage her to be still and let you massage her teeth. Reward her with treats afterwards.

Finally, start wetting the gauze and adding a cleaning agent. You can use baking soda, but commercial toothpastes designed for dogs have flavors dogs are likely to accept (such as chicken)! Focus on cleaning around the gum line. Be very gentle so the gums do not become irritated. Cleaning your dog's teeth once or twice a week should be adequate.

Having said all this, I must say that I have not had complete success cleaning my own dog's teeth. He readily accepts me playing with his mouth and even the gauze, but he's a very active dog and squiggles around so much that I never feel I'm really getting his teeth clean. If this is the case with your puppy, you'll have to rely on your veterinarian to help keep your dog's teeth clean. However, a professional cleaning at the veterinarian's office usually requires general anesthesia. Obviously, it would be preferable to prevent the need for professional cleaning.

Keeping Teeth Clean

You can help reduce tartar buildup on your dog's teeth by routinely giving her crunchy, instead of soft, food and hard dog biscuits and nylon bones to chew. Pedigree makes a dog bone called Dentabone that is supposed to reduce tartar buildup; my dog loves this product. I buy it at my local grocery store. There are chew-type products on the market advertised to help keep the teeth clean, but I have found some dogs can chew these into slimy pieces, which could pose a choking hazard. If you try these, supervise when your dog chews them.

How do we get the odor of skunk off our dog?

There are numerous commercial products on the market now — available at pet stores, veterinary clinics, and through pet catalogs — that are supposed to eliminate skunk odor. Unfortunately, few of us seem to have these on hand when we need them.

An old-fashioned, but messy, remedy is tomato juice. You'll have to soak the dog in it, rub it in, and leave it on for a while, but it often works well. Follow with shampoo and lots of rinsing to get out the tomato juice. If you have no tomato juice on hand, try a vinegar and water solution — about one part vinegar to five parts water.

Should ear cleaning be part of routine grooming? If so, how do we go about cleaning our dog's ears?

Certainly check your dog's ears routinely. Overcleaning can irritate the delicate tissues in the ear, so you only want to clean your puppy's ears if he has excessive wax buildup, develops smelly ears, or has an ear infection that requires treatment.

Even if your dog never needs his ears cleaned, it's a good idea to get him used to your handling his ears by touching them to look inside, and perhaps by touching them with a slightly damp piece of cotton, just in case you ever do need his cooperation for a cleaning.

If you will be routinely cleaning his ears, never use products such as hydrogen peroxide or alcohol, which may be too harsh. Use instead a solution designed for cleaning dogs' ears, which can be purchased from your veterinarian or through pet catalogs. You can also use mineral oil. Soak a piece of cotton with the solution, and very gently wipe out the ear. Or, take a soft tissue, soak it with

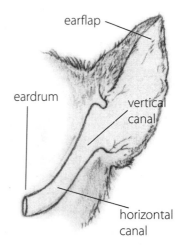

Never try to clean past the vertical part of your dog's ear canal. You could injure the eardrum.

the cleaning solution or mineral oil, wrap it around your little finger, and wipe out the ear. *Never try to clean beyond the part of the ear you can easily reach with your finger or use a cotton swab in the ear canal, because you could injure the dog's eardrum.* You can use a swab to clean out the folds in the dog's ear flap.

If your dog has an ear condition that requires a more thorough cleaning, ask the staff at your veterinary clinic to show you how. In some dogs, it will be necessary to fill the ear with cleaning solution, massage it in at the base of the ear, then wipe it out.

The breeder who sold us our dog suggested we have the puppy's ears cropped. Should we?

Ear cropping is controversial. You might hear from advocates of cropping that it will reduce the likelihood of your dog developing ear infections. It is true that decreased airflow may contribute to the development of ear infections, but there are plenty of floppy-eared dogs that

Ear Infections

Suspect an ear infection if your dog shakes his head, scratches his ears, or holds his head cocked to one side. If you find debris in the ears that resembles coffee grains, suspect mites. Mites are a parasite and can be extremely irritating. The dog's ears need to be thoroughly cleaned and medicated until the mites are destroyed. If you don't clean out the ears first, the medication may not be able to penetrate and won't do much good.

You can buy miticides through catalogs and at pet shops, but I'd go to the veterinarian to be sure you've diagnosed the condition correctly. Some dogs develop bacterial or yeast infections that require additional treatment with other medications.

If not properly treated initially, ear conditions can persist indefinitely, making your dog miserable. They also can lead to more costly treatment down the road if a deep-seated infection develops, which may require general anesthesia to enable the veterinarian to adequately clean out the ear. Another risk is the development of a hematoma, or blood blister, in the flap of the ear if the dog is continually shaking his head due to an ear problem. It's better to pay the veterinarian's bill at the first sign of ear trouble and get the problem resolved promptly.

never have ear problems. The real purpose of ear cropping is to make the dog look a certain way. In short, it's a strictly cosmetic procedure.

Years ago, we always had our Boxer puppies' ears cropped because it was the thing to do. It never occurred to us not to have them cropped. I can tell you that this is not an innocuous procedure. The dog must be anesthetized, and the edges of the ear are cut off and stitched. The ears are then splinted to get them to stand up. We had a few puppies that did not seem to be much bothered by cropping, but we had two that were in significant distress after the procedure. After observing their discomfort, I decided never to have a dog's ears cropped again. It just isn't worth making the dog miserable, and it is not necessary.

In the United States, ear cropping has been traditional for some breeds, such as the Doberman Pinscher, Boxer, and Great Dane. In the United Kingdom, the procedure has been banned. I think the British have the right idea.

If you decide you want the dog's ears cropped, find a veterinarian who is experienced in cropping ears for your breed of dog. Get several recommendations from other dog owners. Do not allow someone who is not a licensed veterinarian to crop your dog's ears. Some states prohibit anyone other than a veterinarian from cropping a dog's ears, as indeed it should be.

Tail docking also is a strictly cosmetic procedure, but many dogs have their tails docked, or cut off, soon after birth; the tail will be gone by the time the puppy goes to its permanent home. Breeds of dog that traditionally have the tail docked include the Doberman Pinscher, Boxer, Rottweiler, Airedale Terrier, toy Poodle, Yorkshire Terrier, and many others.

chapter **8**

Training
Frustrations

Your puppy may already know certain commands before you "adopt" him, or he may have had no training at all. There are many things an owner can do to informally lay the groundwork for formal training (see chapter 11, Training Basics), reinforce training once it has begun, and reduce the likelihood of troublesome behavior (such as unwanted barking or overguarding.)

My small-breed dog slips out of her collar easily. Is there alternative training equipment?

Yes. Buy a halter for the dog, which fits over and around the chest. It's virtually impossible to slip out of a well-fitted halter. A good-quality halter usually can be purchased for under $15.

The disadvantage of the halter is that you'll probably find it harder to control the dog when teaching her to "Heel," since pressure on the chest doesn't seem to have the same impact as pressure put on the neck with a collar. This problem can be alleviated with the following method:

Put on *both* a halter and a collar. Attach the snap on the leash to the ring on the back of the halter, then run the handle end of the leash through the ring on the collar. Pull the leash through, so that the length of leash from halter to collar is not quite taut. Attaching the leash to the halter ensures the dog can't get away if she loses her collar; running the leash through the collar enables you to get her attention with a quick, slight tug on the neck as you teach her to heel. The neck tug, by the way, should never be severe.

With time, the dog will get into the habit of walking nicely by your side and you should be able to get rid of the collar; a slight tug on the halter or a verbal command, such as "wait," should be all you need. If the dog backslides and starts tugging again, go back to using the collar again for a while with the halter.

The combination of halter, collar, and leash can be used to help train small dogs that easily slip out of their collars.

Should I use a choke collar? My large-breed dog often pulls ahead of me on our walks.

Choke collars can be quite useful for training if you use them correctly. First, a few cautionary words. *I would not use a choke collar on a very small breed of dog, or on a young puppy, because you might injure the neck.* Chokes are probably okay for puppies if you have a medium- or large-sized breed and once the dog is about six months old.

As with any collar, a choke must fit correctly; you should be able to just fit two fingers between the collar and the dog's neck. Only use this collar for training. Remove it at all other times, because a choke collar can easily become caught on something and strangle the dog.

Chokes are probably not a good choice for very small dogs that can easily slip out of a collar when the diameter of the head isn't much larger than that of the neck. In such cases, I have found that a choke can come off more readily than a nylon or leather collar, even when fitted properly, because the metal slides easily over a dog's coat. Instead, use the halter/collar combination described above.

The purpose of the choke is to get the dog's attention by compressing the neck for a second. The clinking metal of the choke collar also makes a noise that tells your dog to "Listen up." Here's how to use the choke: When your dog starts to pull ahead, issue a *quick* tug/release to get your point across and at the same time, say "No!" Repeat as necessary until the dog gets the idea.

It is important that you put on the collar correctly so it compresses and releases properly. See the drawing on page 119; if you have trouble figuring out how to get it on, ask a knowledgeable person for help. Your veterinarian's staff or a clerk at a pet shop should be able to help.

With choke collars, you must also avoid inflicting unnecessary pain, which could jeopardize successful training. Dog trainer Bonnie Bergin, demonstrating the proper use of these collars on a television show, made an excellent suggestion: Try the collar on your own arm first to get a good idea of how it will feel on the dog and to get a feel for the intensity you want to apply when issuing a tug/release. *Never tug so hard that you pull the dog off his feet or to the side.*

If you don't like the idea of using a choke, or don't think you can use it safely, information about alternative training equipment appears below — specifically the No-Pull Humane Anti-Tug halter or the Gentle Leader head collar. These products are described below and, frankly, I think are better choices.

What else can I do to keep my dog from pulling while we walk?

Dr. Wayne Hunthausen of Westwood, Kansas, a veterinarian, animal behaviorist, and co-author of *Dog Behavior and Training: Veterinary Advice for Owners,* says he's had great success with the No-Pull Humane Anti-Tug System. This device has a collar that attaches to nylon cords that go under the dog's armpits and compress when the dog tugs. It is available through the *Doctors Foster & Smith* catalog. It doesn't cause pain, and it really gets the dog's attention. Dogs usually stop pulling immediately, Dr. Hunthausen says.

There are other devices on the market that look similar to this product, but compress the chest. I tried one of these and found it did not work especially well, primarily because it didn't fit correctly even though I bought the one recommended for my dog's size. If you want to try this kind of product, I'd stick to the one recommended by Dr. Hunthausen.

What is the device that goes around the nose of dogs that resist training?

This device is a type of head collar that was introduced in 1989. It is called the Gentle Leader (originally the Promise head collar) and was designed by a veterinarian and dog obedience expert. Gentle Leader is recommended by several of the nation's leading veterinarians who specialize in dog behavior. It can help with a wide variety of problems, including the "headstrong" dog that resists training in general, and specific behavior problems, such as excessive barking, jumping up, being aggressive, or pulling uncontrollably on a leash. The manufacturer advertises the product as a device for dogs with an "attitude" problem.

The Gentle Leader head collar usually is sold as part of a system that also includes a training booklet and a dragline (a sort of leash for indoor use). The head collar has two straps: One fits over the dog's nose and one around the neck. When you issue a correction with either the leash or the dragline, it exerts pressure on the back of the dog's neck, where there are strong muscles, as well as on the nose and jaw.

The device is supposed to appeal to a dog's natural instinct to respond to control, because a mother dog often disciplines puppies by applying gentle pressure to the neck, and a leader dog may discipline a pack dog by applying pressure around the nose and lower jaw. If used indoors with the dragline, you can issue a correction from a distance. You can correct the puppy without scolding — and that's good because when you scold a dog, you are still giving the animal attention, even if it is negative. After correcting the dog with the head collar, you can then reward the puppy for good behavior. This process encourages obedience.

When fitted properly with the head collar, the dog can open his mouth to eat, drink, pant, fetch, and bark; when you pull on the attached leash or dragline, the mouth closes. Although the device looks odd compared with a regular collar, the manufacturer of Gentle Leader says the device is not a muzzle and that it is more humane than a choke collar, which puts pressure on the throat and can choke a dog.

There are "copycat" devices on the market, but Gentle Leader's manufacturer maintains these are primarily intended for walking dogs and are not as versatile because they won't work as well indoors.

The Gentle Leader system costs under $30. It may be available through pet stores in your area. It also is sold through veterinarians and trainers, who may charge an additional consultation fee for helping owners with fractious dogs. If you are having serious behavior problems with your puppy, you'll want the input of a veterinarian or trainer anyway.

If you can't find the product in your area and your veterinarian isn't familiar with it, contact the Gentle Leader manufacturer (see the Appendix). The manufacturer also is developing a training video, which eventually will be part of the system (for an added cost) or can be purchased separately.

Some veterinarians and trainers who recommend Gentle Leader say that the device can bring about rapid, dramatic improvement in a dog's behavior. If you have a puppy that's a handful, I think it would be an excellent idea to buy this device. To make sure it works, you need to learn to use it properly and help condition your dog to wear the device.

The Gentle Leader head collar fits around the dog's nose and neck and controls the animal in much the same way his mother or pack leader would. It can be an excellent choice for owners who are having trouble getting their puppies to obey.

I've tried without success to teach my puppy simple commands. Are some dogs just stupid?

Some dogs learn more slowly than others, and some can be just plain stubborn; but there are few dogs that cannot be trained to some extent. Some very young dogs — under six months — will not be able to focus their attention as long as older dogs during "formal" training sessions. You may be expecting too much of the dog. Other dogs have an amazing ability to learn from a very young age.

Next, carefully review your approach to training. Training should be fun. In fact, it should be like a play session. It also needs to be simple so the dog doesn't get confused. When you initiate training, focus on only one command for just a few minutes daily. I'd start with "Sit." Reward the dog with treats, pats, and lots of verbal praise. Do not try to teach the dog another command until she has mastered "Sit."

After she has learned "Sit" and you've practiced it successfully for several days, then move on to "Stay" (see the next question and answer). After she has mastered this command, too, try using both commands during one session. Practice "Sit" several times, then "Stay." Only after she has mastered this task should you try rotating the commands. If she has problems obeying, return to practicing one command at a time.

Be sure you are providing enough repetition. If you work with the dog daily for five to ten minutes, she'll learn a lot faster than if you only work with her two or three times a week for three minutes.

As the dog learns and her attention span improves, expand her learning experience. Gradually add one command at a time and lengthen the time of training sessions. Sessions usually do not need to be more than ten or fifteen minutes daily — or five or ten minutes twice daily, as you choose — and they should never be so long that they become an unwelcome chore for you or the dog.

Always end the training session on a positive note — using a command the dog can easily obey, and if at all possible, follow up with a real play session of fetch or whatever else the dog likes to do. I've found this approach makes the dog more amenable to further training. The dog comes to associate training with an entirely pleasant experience.

If you still have trouble getting the dog to learn commands, enroll yourself and the dog in an obedience class recommended by your veterinarian or your local humane society. The assistance of a professional trainer can do wonders.

My puppy "Stays," but not for more than a second or two. How can I get him to stay put?

If the dog "stays" at all, that's progress! It means the dog already understands the command. As the dog matures, so will his ability to "Stay" for longer periods of time. A young puppy should not be expected to "Stay" for more than several seconds.

Enable your puppy to obey the command. Always have him "Sit" or "Lie down" before asking him to stay in these positions; he'll be more likely to "Stay" than if he's standing. When you tell the dog to "Stay," be sure to use a hand signal because it reinforces your verbal command: Briefly show the dog the palm of your hand as you say "Stay." At first, *do not* walk away. He'll want to follow you and will disobey your command. You want to make it possible for him to obey. When the dog is able to stay for several seconds without you moving, then start trying to take a step or two away from the dog. If he moves, give him a friendly scold, repeat the command, and try again until he gets the message.

My puppy gets "Sit" and "Down" mixed up. How can I get her to differentiate these commands?

Don't scold the dog for trying! If you tell her "Down" and she "Sits," I'd ignore the mistake but physically show her the "Down" command by gently pulling out her front feet while she is sitting. Reward her as soon as she is down. If you ask for "Sit" and she lies down, pull her up onto all fours, then say "Sit" as you push her back legs under and hold a treat up over her head to encourage the correct position.

Return to practicing each command separately. Try the two together only after she has mastered each command individually, as explained above.

Our puppy won't "Come" when called unless it's his dinnertime. How can we make him listen?

Practicing the "Come" command, with a long leash if necessary as described in chapter 11, certainly will help. Use treats to practice having the dog "Come" to you elsewhere in the house or out in the yard. Don't use treats every single time, however. Use a treat the first time or two; then the next time the dog obeys, reward him with very generous pats on the head and verbal praise, or some play. Make it like a game, and do it again and again. You want the dog to associate "Come" with a very pleasant experience.

There are other ways to make sure a dog obeys the "Come" command. Never call the dog to you to scold or correct him. Go to the dog instead to issue a correction. If the dog learns that "Come" means an unpleasant reprimand from the owner, then "Come" won't be something he'll want to do.

Our puppy obeys commands only if we have his favorite treat in hand. What should we do?

Whether or not to use treats for training has been a subject of controversy among trainers for years for this very reason. Some dogs trained with food treats just won't obey unless they are offered treats. Other trainers believe treats are an invaluable training aid.

The answer probably lies somewhere in between. Start out with treats, simply because it makes training so much easier. Then rotate food treats with other types of praise — pats on the head and very enthusiastic verbal praise. At the end of a training session, play the dog's favorite game as further reward. I can't stress enough how important it is to make training fun for the dog. If the dog learns that obeying his owner results in some playful interaction, he's far more likely to obey.

Our puppy obeys commands at home, but not anywhere else. What can we do?

Your puppy has formed the habit of obeying at home but hasn't formed the habit of obeying anywhere else. Start conducting training sessions in different places. First, select a place that is different but that doesn't have too many distractions, such as a relative or neighbor's quiet backyard.

Begin with one command at a time. Take along your dog's favorite treat. Once you have him paying attention in this place, move on to another, and yet another. I used to have a neighbor who took her dogs across the street to a shopping center (on leash), where she trained them. You'll also gradually need to increase the distractions presented to the dog. See the next question and answer.

My puppy "Heels" until there is a distraction, then she tries to take off!

Training a dog to obey despite distractions is one of the more difficult aspects of training. It takes persistence. Intentionally expose your dog to distractions so you have the opportunity to teach her that she must obey despite activity around her. For instance, ask a friend or neighbor to come around the corner as you are walking the dog. When the dog starts to lunge or bolt, give a sharp "No!" along with a slight jerk on her collar to get her attention, then keep her walking next to you. Reward her with a treat when she starts listening and obeying your command to "Heel." This has to be done again and again.

It will take time before your dog continues to heel for longer periods of time. Once you train her to obey you with this exercise, try a stronger distraction. See if you can get a friend with a dog to show up during your outing.

Remember that some distractions will prove too tempting even for a well-trained dog. A dog might get used to the distraction of other people and dogs or to squirrels and birds in the vicinity and learn to obey you despite them; but if something new, such as a deer, suddenly shows up, she might try to take off again. That's why it's imperative to keep your dog leashed any time she isn't in the house or in a securely fenced-in backyard.

I encouraged my puppy to bark because I want a good guard dog, but now she barks too much.

This is a difficult problem, because you want the dog to issue necessary warnings. When you are home and the dog barks in response to a noise, go and investigate, give the dog a small pat on the head, then immediately ask her in a matter-of-fact manner to come along with you and distract her with some other activity. You don't want to punish her for barking in this instance, nor do you want to "overreward" her. Sometimes, acknowledging a dog's warning bark will get her to stop.

When she barks inappropriately and you are home, tell her "No!" If necessary, put her on a leash and keep her with you so you can issue "No" at appropriate times. Wait until after she has been quiet for a while, and then reward her with a pat on the head for being quiet. You could try adverse conditioning, but use this only as a last resort. You could shake coins in a can or squirt the dog with a water gun, for example, for inappropriate barking.

If the dog is barking when you are out, you may have to do a little detective work to figure out why she is barking. Ask a neighbor to help you pinpoint the cause, or try leaving a tape recorder on to see how much she is barking and if you can pick up any sounds that might be setting her off. Here are some examples of situations you may not realize can cause dogs to bark and some practical solutions:

- **Trash collectors.** Set the trash cans farther away from the house. Also close shades or curtains, shut windows when possible, and leave on the television or radio, so the puppy is less likely to notice the trash crew.

- **People walking by the house.** Shut shades or curtains and close windows to block out sights, and leave on the television or radio to mute sounds.

- **In apartments, people walking down the hall.** This can especially be a problem if there is a gap under your front door that enables the puppy to see and hear people going down the hall. Try blocking the gap with a towel. If the design of your home allows, block the hall-way to the front door with a baby gate.

- **At night, reflections in windows.** My dog seldom barks, except when he sees reflections at night in the glass. Shutting the shades stops the barking.

- **The dark.** Some dogs don't like being left alone, especially when the lights are out. Leave a light on for your puppy. If it gets dark before you come home from work, invest in a timer that will automatically turn on a light at dusk.

- **Separation anxiety.** Some dogs bark when they become anxious over being left alone. If you think this is the case, refer to the infor-mation on separation anxiety in chapter 1, and condition the dog to your absences.

Don't forget to enlist the help of a neighbor or leave on a tape recorder to see if your efforts to stop unwelcome barking are successful.

If the dog is barking when you go out and it is not caused by separa-tion anxiety, and you truly believe there is no good reason for her behav-ior, resort to adverse conditioning. Pretend you are going out the front door. Wait for the dog to start barking. When she does, immediately come in and tell her "NO NO!!" You'll have to do this many, many times.

Don't forget to enlist the help of your veterinarian or professional trainer if you can't seem to get this problem under control. Sometimes, an outsider can figure out what's making a dog bark and what to do about it when you can't!

Are there devices that can help stop a puppy from barking?

Yes. There is a relatively new kind of collar that sprays citronella under the dog's chin when he barks. It's called the ABS Collar and is available from some veterinarians and can be purchased through the *R. C. Steele* catalog (see Appendix).

Dr. Hunthausen cautions that this is a form of adverse conditioning and should be used only when other methods fail. Nor should adverse conditioning be used on a puppy with separation anxiety, which could make matters worse. But when Dr. Hunthausen has recommended the use of this collar for barking behavior, the results have been excellent, he says.

"It's not just the scent. It's the feel of the spray, the sight of the spray, and the sound," says Dr. Hunthausen. He has found that dogs learn not to bark when the collar is on, because they associate the presence of the collar with something unpleasant, but that they will sometimes continue to bark when the collar is off. This can be good for owners who want their dog to bark at certain times. If owners want their dogs to bark when they aren't home as a deterrent to burglars they leave the collar off. If they don't want them to bark when they are home, they put the collar on.

Are electronic shock collars a good way to stop excessive barking and other problem behaviors?

There are different kinds of shock collars on the market. One type operates with a remote control and enables you to issue a shock when the dog barks or does something else you don't want him to. Obviously, this kind of shock collar requires your presence. Another kind of electronic shock collar responds to the dog's bark — if the dog barks once, he does not get a shock; if he continues barking, he does.

With some of these collars, the intensity of the shock can be varied. Some manufacturers compare the shock to static electricity. Although shock collars are recommended by some dog trainers, their use is controversial, and some consider them inhumane.

Dr. Richard H. Polsky, of Animal Behavior Counseling Services, Inc., Los Angeles, writes in the *Journal of the American Animal Hospital Association* that shock collars can rapidly suppress some behaviors, such as excessive barking. But he has found several disadvantages based on many hours of hands-on experience One is the random discharge of shock, which he calls a "serious and surprisingly common problem." With remote collars, the cause is often an extraneous radio signal coming from something other than the collar's transmitter. Automatic antibark collars also are prone to misfire, he says.

To be effective, shock collars must be used with appropriate intensity (which varies among dogs), at the right time, and for the correct duration. If they are used inappropriately — or if they discharge when they shouldn't — the dog is going to become confused, possibly traumatized, and probably afraid of the environment where the shock occurs. Some dogs may regress after the collar is removed, and others may become aggressive in response to the shock. Skin abrasion on the neck also can result from the electrodes on the collars, this behaviorist says.

Dr. Polsky concludes that shock collars should only be used when all other options have failed. The decision to use a shock collar should be made on a case-by-case basis and only by people experienced with this kind of product. *They are inappropriate for dogs with separation anxiety, dogs that have phobias to loud noises, or dogs that misbehave because of fear,* he says.

Personally, I wouldn't use one of these devices unless it was absolutely the last resort. If you have a dog with a barking problem, try the techniques described earlier in this chapter; if they don't work, call in a professional trainer recommended by your local humane society or veterinarian.

Our puppy is adorable now but is considered an "aggressive breed." Can we train her to be nice?

Virtually any dog can become aggressive, but several breeds of dogs may be more likely than others to do so because they were derived from fighting dogs or have been bred to guard. These include Chow Chows, German Shepherd dogs, Rottweilers, dogs of the breeds commonly referred to as pit bulls, and Doberman Pinschers.

Each and every one of these dogs make lovely pets if they are socialized and trained. If they are not, you could have a disaster on your hands, not only because of their breed but because they are larger, more powerful dogs. They can do a lot more damage than a ferocious Chihuahua. As the owner of this type of dog, you have a responsibility even more so than other dog owners to make sure the dog is socialized and trained.

The types of and reasons for aggressive problems vary, but they can be caused by such instinctive canine behavior as guarding or pack instinct. Let me give you an example of each:

Example 1: When my grandmother became elderly, she lived in a private home with two other older women. The owner of the home acquired a beautiful German Shepherd puppy. Because some of the women in the house were debilitated, they didn't go out much, and when they did, they seldom took the dog.

Consequently, the dog spent all his time around the house and was seldom exposed to strangers. He got along famously with the women and became quite protective. He would bark ferociously when a stranger came around, whether the person was male or female, young or old. As he got older, the owner had to lock the dog in a back room if anyone the dog didn't know came in.

One day, a repairman came to the front door and the owner mistakenly assumed the dog was locked in the back room, but he wasn't. He raced out, through the living room, out the open front door, and attacked the repairman. He took out a chunk of flesh over the repairman's ribs. Thankfully, the injuries weren't too bad, but they did require medical treatment. There was the threat of a lawsuit. Home owners' insurance paid the bills, but the company made it clear it would not pay for any further incidents caused by the dog. A veterinarian considered the dog a time bomb and advised that the dog be euthanized. The owner, fearing another incident, ended up giving the dog away, rather than have the dog put to sleep or take the chance she might go broke if the dog attacked someone else, and she was successfully sued.

Example 2: A tragic incident in my area a few years ago was widely reported on in the local media. A family had two Rottweilers. One day, the dogs escaped and viciously attacked a woman innocently walking down the sidewalk. Her injuries were severe, requiring many stitches, and the dogs were confiscated by authorities. The neighbors claimed the dogs spent a lot of time together in the backyard or in the garage. If the reports were accurate, they indicate that these animals spent little time in the house with people. And if you have two dogs of a potentially aggressive breed instead of one, the possibility for trouble rises, because pack instincts take over.

Now a few words about how to avoid these kinds of problems. All dogs, especially guard-type dogs, need to be routinely exposed to people. They should live in the home, with their family. They should be frequently taken on walks, starting from the time they are puppies, and exposed to other people in all types of situations. That means taking them for walks in your own neighborhood on leash, repeatedly introducing them to neighbors, and taking them anywhere else you can think of. They must learn obedience training, which makes them less likely to get out of hand.

Some people believe they have to raise their dogs to hate strangers to make sure the dogs will guard their family, but this isn't true. A friendly family pet is still likely to bark and protect the family if an intruder comes around.

I also advise that anyone with one of these breeds protect their dog from people who might be quick to accuse the animal of a misdeed, even when one didn't really happen. If your dog ever leaves a mark on anyone with his teeth — which can happen innocently when puppies and children play together and go for a toy at the same time — you could find an irate parent accusing your dog of being vicious, even if you know he isn't. Generally, do not let your dog play with children outside the family, and especially with young children, who are likely to pull tails, ears, and pound on the dog, provoking an incident. If you have very young children of your own, always supervise when the children and dog are together.

What are the signs of an aggressive dog?

Dogs that are dominant aggressive generally bare their teeth and hold up their ears and tails. Dogs that act aggressive as a result of fear may show their teeth but generally keep their ears flat to their head and their tails down. Each type of aggression needs to be handled differently. Dominant aggressive dogs often need lots of obedience training with positive reinforcement. Dogs with fear aggression may respond best to gradual conditioning to the things that make them afraid. If your dog demonstrates any type of aggression, consult an expert. This is not a problem that average dog owners should try to handle on their own.

Are underground electric fences a good way to train our puppy to stay in the yard?

These devices work in much the same manner as the collars designed to train dogs not to bark inappropriately, and they have some of the same problems as described above. The dog wears a collar, and when he comes within five or ten feet of an underground wire, he gets a shock. Some of these collars are supposed to warn the dog first with a sound before the animal is shocked.

A major problem with these devices is that owners often don't realize they still have to put in a good bit of time training their dog to use this kind of system. Otherwise it is unlikely to work.

The boundary of the yard where the wire is buried needs to be marked with flags to help the dog learn just where the boundary is. The owner should work with the dog on a leash to train him not to go beyond that boundary by walking him up to the boundary and then issuing a jerk *away* and a "No!" This should be done several times daily for many days and, sometimes, for weeks before the message sinks in. And you must be consistent. Don't work with the puppy for a couple times a day, then let him loose in the yard to get shocked later.

Without this kind of training, the dog could bolt over the boundary in his attempt to escape the shock. I also think that some of the collars that come with these systems are bulky and are likely to be uncomfortable for a dog to wear all the time. However, if you don't use the collar all the time, you might forget to put it back on before the dog goes outside.

If this kind of system is in good working order, and if dogs are appropriately trained by their owners, it can be an excellent way to contain a dog in a yard. Manufacturers claim these systems also are cheaper than conventional fencing. Personally, I have more faith in a solid, physical barrier. But if you can't afford a traditional fence, you live in an area that forbids one, and you are willing to put in the time it takes to train the dog to adjust to the electric fence, it could be a good option.

Our puppy jumps up on people, especially guests. How can we get her to stop?

This is your dog's way of greeting guests, but jumping up can be a bad habit and could pose a risk to children and the elderly if she knocks them over. Ask her to "Sit," and kneel down with her. Put on her collar and leash, if necessary. Hold her still, using the "Stay" command, and ask your guests to squat if possible and pat the dog. Ask a cooperative friend or neighbor to help you train the dog by coming to the door so you can practice. The dog needs to form the habit of sitting when guests arrive.

Another method of handling a dog that jumps up is to have the person she's greeting raise his or her knee to block the dog. The goal is not to knock the dog over or down; it's just to get the message across that jumping up does not get the dog the greeting she is seeking, and a knee block to the chest is a bit unpleasant. This technique might work if it's you the dog is jumping up on because you can practice; but for guests, it is not very practical.

Here's a method that the owner of a boisterous Labrador Retriever found to be effective: When the dog jumped up, she squeezed the dog's front paws just enough to make the dog uncomfortable.

We want our dog to guard us when we answer the door, but she overdoes it and charges at guests.

This problem must be stopped because it's not only unpleasant for guests, but the dog might just charge right out the door if given the opportunity or become aggressive toward people coming to the door.

As with jumping up, dogs that charge the door should be taught to "Sit" when someone comes to the door. Teach them to sit several feet back and to the side of the door; it's close enough to be threatening to a possibly unwelcome guest, but far enough away so that the dog is less likely to go right out the door.

You can practice teaching the dog to sit for the doorbell simply by ringing it yourself, then asking the dog to "Sit, Stay," and then rewarding the dog. Then have friends or neighbors help by coming to the door so you can continue practicing.

The other solution is to put the dog on a leash before you open the door, and teach the dog to "Sit, Stay" right next to you. This might be preferable if you want the dog closer to you when you open the door.

Is there a way to train our puppy not to be afraid of thunderstorms?

This is not uncommon in dogs, and no one really knows for sure why some dogs fear thunderstorms and others do not. The degree of fright varies widely. A friend of mine has a Poodle mix named Muffin. The dog associates rain with thunder; if a drop of rain falls from the sky, she starts to tremble and runs to hide. Yet this same dog will jump into a water trough on a hot day to cool herself off.

In other dogs, a thunderstorm can set off uncontrollable panic behavior. I have in mind a Labrador Retriever that goes absolutely wild during storms and runs around the house in a panic, wrecking the place in the process.

Veterinarian and animal behaviorist Nicholas Dodman says that thunderstorm phobias actually are uncommon in puppies and are more often seen in older dogs. When a young dog begins to show fear of thunderstorms, however, it is wise to take steps immediately to prevent a full-blown phobia from developing.

I would avoid comforting your dog during thunderstorms. This might promote the fear behavior, because in a way you are rewarding her for being afraid. Use positive conditioning instead. Every time there's a thunderstorm, act like a wonderful event is occurring and give your puppy treats during each "boom." Be forewarned that the positive results may wear off if you don't keep up the routine, or at least reinforce it periodically.

Many trainers recommend using a tape recording of thunderstorms to gradually condition dogs to the sound, along

Dog Psychology

To learn more about the psychology of dogs — and at the same time, give yourself a good read — obtain a copy of Dr. Dodman's book *The Dog Who Loved Too Much*. Dr. Dodman relates some fascinating tales and, in the process, helps owners understand their dogs. He also gives lots of concrete advice about how to deal with a variety of behavior problems.

with positive conditioning as described above. The use of a tape is handy, since you can play it at any time and you can't predict when real storms will occur. Play the tape at a lower level at first and for only several seconds, and provide positive experiences such as verbal praise and treats. If the dog seems to be tolerating the noise, gradually increase the sound and length of time the tape plays. This method takes a lot of effort on the part of the owner. It will work very well with some dogs and might not with others. It is certainly worth trying.

If you have a dog that doesn't respond to any of these methods, and her behavior becomes extreme, you'll have to go out of your way to make sure the dog is not left alone during thunderstorms until you seek professional help. If you must go out and leave the dog alone during thunderstorm season, leave on televisions or radios in rooms where the dog goes to help mask out the sound. A less viable option is to drop the dog off at a helpful neighbor's during these times, or have someone come to stay with the dog.

Our puppy cries and whines after we go to bed, because he wants to sleep in the bedroom with us.

You'll have to tough it out. This is typical behavior for puppies that have just come home with their new owners. Think about it. They were with their mother and their littermates and now suddenly find themselves alone in a strange place. What else can you expect?

Be sure you've provided a comfortable, safe place for your puppy to sleep (see chapter 10). Never place a puppy in a dark basement or lock him in a tiny room with the door closed, such as the bathroom. Instead, you might select the kitchen or a hallway. Put up a safe baby gate that will keep him in his "space" but allows him to see out. For a bed, a cardboard box (with no staples or other hazardous materials) can be used. Line it with a soft blanket that has no fringe or other loose material the puppy could ingest.

To comfort a new puppy, some owners place a hot water bottle and an alarm clock under the blankets. The hot water bottle is supposed to simulate the warmth of the puppy's mother; the clock simulates her heartbeat. (The hot water bottle must have a secure fastener so the water can't leak out and burn the puppy.)

When the puppy starts to cry and whine, you must ignore the behavior, which eventually should stop. This is common advice given by many trainers who advise against letting your puppy sleep in your bedroom or on your bed. More on that appears in the next question.

Personally, I believe in letting dogs into the bedroom and, in fact, wouldn't have it any other way. I can't bear the sound of a puppy in distress. Anytime I've had a new puppy, I put him in a box with proper bedding next to my bed, where I can pat and reassure him from time to time. Consequently, I haven't had a problem with whining or crying. When the puppy grows larger, I let him sleep on my bed.

I was told that if I let my dog sleep with me, he won't obey me. Is this true?

As mentioned above, some trainers advise against letting your dog sleep with you. They believe that the dog will view you more as an equal pack member instead of his master, and that consequently it will be more difficult to get him to obey you. These trainers say it will also make it harder for the dog to learn to be alone when you go out. On the other hand, many owners let their dogs sleep on the bed or in the bedroom, and they have no problem.

It may not be a good idea if you are having problems teaching your puppy to obey you or stay home alone without destroying your house. I do believe, however, that a dog should be allowed to at least sleep in the same room of a family member. It's nice for the dog and the family to be near one another. There also was a study conducted some years ago by the Monks of New Skete, well-known dog trainers and authors of *How to Be Your Dog's Best Friend*. In over 400 cases of problem dogs they studied, 80 percent slept outside of their owners' bedrooms. These trainers say that letting the dog sleep in your room builds trust and confidence between pet and owner. I especially believe that puppies left alone all day should be with their owners as much as possible when their owners are home, since too much isolation is not good for dogs. Dogs are pack animals, and you and your family are your dog's pack.

Perhaps most important is to make a decision and stick to it. You cannot let a puppy get used to sleeping with you, then kick him out of bed. It is not fair to the dog, and he is likely to keep you up for nights crying or howling to get back in bed. If your puppy will grow to be a very large dog, and you suspect that in the future you will not want him in bed because he'll take up too much room, then start training him now to sleep in his own bed on the floor next to you.

A cautionary note: Some small-breed puppies are so tiny that it might not be safe to let them sleep with you until they grow larger. They might become injured or suffocate if you roll over on them.

Puppy Owner Problems

You may have done everything a responsible pet owner can possibly do to make life with your puppy go smoothly, but at times certain unexpected situations arise. What happens when you're overly busy and stressed out? When a family member develops allergies? When you have to go out of town for a few days or move to a new location? Finding appropriate temporary supervision, a long-term pet sitter, or an entirely new home for your dog will require careful planning, research, and follow-up on your part.

I love our new puppy, but sometimes I get angry and yell when he doesn't obey. Is this harmful?

Yelling at a puppy can have a variety of effects. Some breeds of dogs, such as the Italian Greyhound or the Whippet, are known to be sensitive to harsh words. Yelling could cause the dogs to withdraw and become timid. Such dogs will cower or go off and hide. They could become nervous. In other dogs, yelling doesn't have much impact; they become accustomed to it and before long, will ignore you. Yet other dogs might respond aggressively, although I suspect this is uncommon.

Most puppy owners will occasionally get angry at their new pets and yell, because puppies can tax your patience, just as children can. I certainly have yelled "STOP CHASING THE CATS!!" more times than I can count. If you only occasionally yell at the dog and it doesn't seem to have much impact, it's probably not going to do him any real harm.

Sometimes a really loud, stern voice is appropriate if it is intended to issue a serious correction for repetitive, inappropriate behavior or if the purpose is to stop your puppy from doing something dangerous, such as running into the street. But in most cases, yelling is not necessary and doesn't do much good either.

To help prevent unnecessary yelling, consider whether you may be expecting too much of your puppy too soon. Allot enough time to work with him on obedience training. If you are stressed because you are having trouble spending enough time with your new pet, get some help. You could hire a dog walker to exercise the dog, since lack of exercise also contributes to mischief-making and disobedience.

Also try to identify the specific things he does that set you off and either plan an appropriate response ahead of time, so you are prepared, or find a way to prevent the problem. If he's getting into the laundry hamper, for instance, and you are angry because he doesn't listen when you tell him "No," put the hamper in a place he can't get to in order to stop this aggravation. In my case, I stopped the dog from chasing my two very elderly cats by separating him from the cats with baby gates. I also now let the cats up on a table that used to be forbidden to them so they can be near me without being terrorized by the dog.

Some days we're too busy to spend time with our dog and we wonder if we should keep him.

First ask yourself if you are meeting the dog's basic needs. Is he being fed properly, and are his health care needs being met? Is he getting exercise daily? Does he seem content when he is left alone? Does he refrain from tearing up the house or soiling inappropriately when you are out? And does he seem happy to see the family when they come home? If your answer to these questions is yes, chances are he's doing fine.

If you are meeting the dog's basic needs but you fear he needs more companionship, consider getting him a "pet." Two dogs keep each other company quite nicely. Some dogs take to cats, if they are raised with them from a very young age. Alternatively, hire a dog walker to take him for a stroll on days the family is going to be out or very busy and unable to spend any time with the dog.

Dogs that are not getting enough attention can become depressed. You can tell because they act lethargic and don't show much interest in anything. They mope. They may develop behavior problems, such as soiling in the house, which could occur because they are anxious — or because they are not being taken outside as often as they need to go. If this is the case, and you cannot see a way to meet your dog's needs, then you should consider finding the dog a better home. To see how, read on.

My new job requires that I move, and I can't take my puppy. How do I find her a good, new home?

Give yourself plenty of time. If you have a purebred dog, a good place to start is with a dog club for that breed. Some are "rescue clubs." Your local humane society should be able to put you in touch with such clubs. If you have a Scottish Terrier, for instance, there is likely to be a Scottish Terrier club in your area or the nearest metropolitan area. People in these clubs have a special interest in certain dog breeds, and they might be able to help you find a good home for your dog or at least give you some guidance.

Also ask your veterinarian. Many veterinary clinics help clients place dogs.

You could resort to advertising, but proceed *very* cautiously if you do. Unfortunately, there are people who pretend they want to take your dog as a pet, only to sell it later to a medical laboratory. Some of them may bring a child in tow to convince you they are a family. One of their sources for finding dogs is the want ads. Unless potential new owners are recommended by someone you know and trust, I would not let them have the dog. If advertising is your only option, and someone responds, visit their home and speak to their neighbors to get a sense of whether they are what they say they are. Ask if they have had dogs previously, for how long they had each dog, and what happened to each dog. Ask for recommendations from a veterinarian, clergy, a boss, or anyone else you can think of.

Once you find a new home for your dog, don't just drop him off the day you leave. Take him to visit his new home several times. Let him get to know his new owners gradually, while you are present. Let him visit there without you once or twice. This will increase the likelihood that he will adjust to his new home and that he will not develop a behavior problem in response to the change — which will increase the likelihood that his new owners will want to keep him always.

I would also ask the new owners to sign a contract stating that if they cannot keep the dog, he is to be returned to you (or a designated person since you'll be out of the country). People who really want the best for animals will not object. My dog's breeder requires all buyers of her puppies to sign such a contract. Here's why: She once sold a puppy to a man she thought would give the dog a good home, only to find out later he had sold or given the dog to a "puppy mill" type of facility, where dogs are kept in often inhumane conditions strictly to breed. The purpose of these places is to produce as many puppies as possible for sale, so the owners can make money. This breeder tried to get the dog back, but couldn't. If more breeders and owners who have to find their dogs new homes required such a contract, fewer animals would end up in bad places.

> If you have to give your puppy away, keep in touch with the new owners routinely to make sure everything is going well and so you can intervene if it isn't!

My well-behaved puppy is lonely because I'm no longer home during the day. Should I keep her?

If you don't work too far from home, consider coming home for lunch, even if it's only three days a week. You could hire someone to walk her at midday on the other days or some days. Professionals in my area charge about $10 per walk, which can add up, so you might want to hire a dog walker for just a couple days a week to keep the bill down.

An option is to find a neighbor who would walk the dog for less; some retired persons would enjoy an outing and the chance to earn a few extra dollars. Or consider asking a retired senior or trustworthy neighbor to actually keep your dog for you during the day. Perhaps you could provide some service in return, such as baby-sitting on weekends. More about finding dog-sitters appears later in this chapter. In some areas, there actually are "doggie day care" facilities, but they are still few and far between.

Yet another option is to get another dog. It could be an older, well-behaved animal. Some puppies and kittens get along very well, especially if they are raised together. You would have a bigger bill for pet food, not to mention the cost of health care for another pet, but it would provide your dog with a companion and provide you with peace of mind.

If you have a lonely puppy, sometimes the best solution is to get him a companion — or two.

My husband is allergic to our son's new puppy. Is there an alternative to getting rid of her?

Yes, there are alternatives. One of the most important steps you can take is to keep the dog out of your bedroom. After all, adults who work out of the home spend a large portion of their time sleeping when they are at home. If necessary, keep the dog out of other rooms in the house where your husband spends a lot of time.

People who are allergic to pets usually are reacting to dog dander (small pieces of skin that have been shed) and saliva. Have your husband experiment to see if he reacts after petting the dog, especially if he pets her and then touches his face. If so, he may need to avoid touching the dog.

There also are products you can buy to treat your puppy that are supposed to help minimize allergic symptoms in people. One is Allerpet, a liquid product that can be ordered through pet catalogs. I've had no need to try these products and have heard conflicting information about whether or not they work. I'd say they certainly are worth a try.

Allergy Control

Is someone in your home sneezing and sniffling in response to your dog or to dust mites? Here are some widely recommended methods of controlling allergies.

Bathe your dog more frequently. Between baths, try rinsing the dog in plain water, which can keep the dander down. Some people believe that using distilled water is better than regular tap water.

Groom your dog more often outdoors or perhaps in a basement, away from the main living areas.

Eliminate allergens from the bedroom. In addition to forbidding the dog from the bedroom, remove any carpet from the room (and elsewhere in the house if necessary), as well as curtains and other dust- and dander-catchers.

Keep the bedroom meticulously clean and as free of dust as possible.

Invest in plastic covers for the mattress and pillows, since they harbor dust mites. Toss out feather pillows and buy the washable, hypoallergenic kind.

Wash bedclothes and pillows frequently in hot water, which will kill dust mites and get rid of any pet dander that might be present.

Keep humidity in the house low, which helps control the dust mite population.

You might also invest in an air-cleaner for the bedroom; be sure to buy the kind with a HEPA (High-Efficiency Particulate Air) filter. There are also more expensive air-cleaning devices that will filter air throughout the house.

Invest in a vacuum cleaner that keeps dust from blowing back out all over the house, which is what happens when you use a regular vacuum cleaner! These newer vacuums are more widely available than before through stores and catalogs.

There are many other commonly recommended methods of controlling allergies. The box above has several suggestions.

Keep in mind that people who have allergies usually react to more than one allergen. Allergy to dust mites, for instance, is even more common than allergy to dogs and cats. Sometimes dogs (and cats) take all the blame, when in fact there are other things in the house contributing to allergic symptoms.

Last but not least, find an allergist for your husband who is willing to establish ways to keep the allergies under control despite the presence of the dog. Of course, some people have more serious conditions (such as asthma, which can be induced by allergies), and a physician may have no choice but to advise finding your puppy a new home. But if your husband's allergy isn't too severe, look for an allergist who appreciates the important role that pets play in our lives and will work with you. Some doctors may be too quick to advise getting rid of a beloved pet without trying alternatives. Don't forget to discuss the situation with your veterinarian, who also may be able to help.

I don't know what to do with my puppy when I go out of town.

Deciding how to arrange for care for your puppy while you are out of town requires special consideration. Puppies tend to be rambunctious and need to be in an especially safe environment where they can't hurt themselves and where they are supervised by someone who will take special care to make sure they cannot escape. There are several possibilities:

- **Consider asking a relative, friend, or neighbor to keep your puppy for you in their home.** It obviously should be a dog lover and one who has experience caring for dogs. I'd be hesitant to ask anyone with a hectic household and very young children; it's too easy for kids to forget and let the puppy out. And again, it must be someone who you feel confident would be sure to look out for your puppy's safety.

  You'll have to decide based on your relationship with a sitter who is a friend or relative whether to offer money, or bring them a nice gift as a thank you. If there is no friend, relative, or neighbor you can ask, here are several other methods of finding a sitter:

- **If you got your puppy from a breeder, ask if he or she would puppy-sit.** Many breeders offer to keep dogs they've bred, often for free, simply because they like to stay involved with dogs they've sold.

- **Hire a pet-sitter who stays at your house while you are gone.** This is a good arrangement because the dog is in a familiar environment and has everything he needs to be comfortable and remain safe. It's also nice to have someone in the house while you are away as a deterrent to burglars.

One problem I've had is that people who love pets and make good pet-sitters usually have pets of their own that need care, which may prevent them from accepting your request. If you find a sitter with a dog that gets along with your puppy, perhaps she could bring her pet along.

■ **Board your puppy at a kennel or dog "hotel."** More information about finding a pet-sitter and a kennel appears below.

Do you have advice about how to find a good pet-sitter?

You can find pet-sitters just by keeping your eyes and ears open and by asking, or by advertising if necessary. One teenager I hired was a neighbor whose family had dogs, so it seemed logical to ask her mother if she could house-sit. My all-time favorite pet-sitter is a 73-year-old retired nurse, Peggy. She lives on a small farm owned by her daughter, who boards one of my horses. Peggy was used to animals, I could see she liked them, and she was obviously a responsible person, too. Again, I simply asked if she'd be interested, and she was. If you need to look beyond friends and family, here are some avenues you might pursue:

■ **Contact local senior citizens groups,** or put up a notice in a local retirement community.

■ **Advertise at a local college.** Even better, ask a teacher or administrator at the college to recommend a responsible student or staff member.

■ **Contact local elementary and high schools,** and ask if you can put up an ad in the teachers' lounge. You might find a teacher who would like to earn some extra money.

- **Advertise in a local newspaper.** I once found an excellent sitter in this way, but exercise caution! Remember, there are people who look for just this kind of ad because they want to obtain dogs to sell to medical laboratories. Interview very carefully, get references, and check out each and every one!

- **Call local veterinary clinics,** and ask if they have any veterinary technicians on staff whom they would recommend to pet-sit on the side.

- **Contact a professional pet-sitting service.** This is likely to be more expensive than hiring a neighborhood college student, because a pet-sitting business is paying for liability insurance and for bonding its employees, but it's an option.

In addition, most professional pet-sitters only visit your house to care for the dog while you are gone; they do not move in. This isn't an arrangement I would select for a puppy, so look for a professional pet-sitting company that has people who will stay at your house overnight.

Pet-sitting services advertise in the Yellow Pages and in local newspapers, but I'd ask a veterinarian or local humane society to recommend one. You can get more information about finding a professional pet-sitter and help in locating one in your area by contacting the National Association of Professional Pet-Sitters. The organization's address and phone number appear in the Appendix.

Once you find someone you think would be a good sitter, talk with her (my sitters have primarily been women) a few times to make sure she is a good candidate. Have her meet your puppy. Watch how she and the puppy interact, and if they seem to like one another.

Ask her to go along with you to take the dog for a walk so you can show her where you walk, where the dog is used to going to the "bathroom," how to clean up after the dog if necessary, and the commands the dog understands. Be sure to let her walk the dog part of the way to determine if you think she can handle the dog. If the dog is used to sleeping in your bedroom, ask the candidate if she is willing to have the puppy there too, or perhaps in the guest room, if that's where she will sleep. I've found that real animal lovers don't mind this request at all and that good pet-sitters want to do everything they can to treat your puppy just as you do.

Ask yourself if the candidate is a take-charge kind of person who would be determined not to let the dog get loose, and who could handle an emergency. The sitter should have some experience with puppies. Otherwise, she won't appreciate all the care that puppies require and won't realize just how careful one must be to safeguard a puppy.

How do I go about training a pet-sitter once I find one I like?

Clearly explain that the number one priority is protecting the puppy's safety and making sure the dog never escapes. Show her whatever security measures you have in place. For instance, the sitter may need to check the lock on the backyard gate to be sure it isn't left open by the trash collectors. Also explain care for the animal, and provide everything in writing. If the sitter doesn't drive or doesn't have a car, discuss how the sitter would get the puppy to the veterinarian's in case of an emergency — it may be necessary to have a backup arrangement. A list of additional information you should provide appears on page 151.

With adolescent pet-sitters, I've found it is important to set rules, such as "no guests in the house," to reduce the likelihood that the sitter will be distracted from caring for the dog, or that there would ever be an "incident" between the dog and a stranger in the house. I've also found that teenaged sitters and young adults often want to be out with their friends instead of doing what you are paying them to do — stay home with your puppy. Give a clear job description so there are no misunderstandings or mishaps; state exactly the hours you expect the sitter to be in your home.

Once you find a good pet-sitter, go out of your way to make your home comfortable for her so she'll come back. Make sure the house is picked up, and leave clean sheets on the bed and fresh towels in the bathroom. Show the sitter around the house so she can easily locate extra toilet paper or tissues, light bulbs, and candles (if it's summertime and storms are likely to cause power outages). Leave some basics in the kitchen, such as coffee, bread, some snacks, and sodas. If you have hired a teenager or elderly individual who doesn't drive, you may have to leave a fully stocked kitchen.

I introduce each sitter to the neighbors so she feels there is someone she can reach quickly in case of an emergency, and who also has an extra set of keys to the house, just in case the sitter accidently locks herself out.

While I'm away, I call home just about everyday to see how the pets are doing and to answer any questions the sitter may have about where to find things in the house or about pet care. This is also a way to check and be sure the sitter is where she's supposed to be.

I encourage the sitter to call me with questions if she has any. I also let my veterinarian's office know that I'm going out of town and that someone else will be keeping my pets, so the staff will be "tuned in" in case the sitter has to call them. I leave a letter for the sitter authorizing treatment if an emergency arises.

It usually costs me $20 a day for in-home pet-sitting. College students are often delighted to get $100 for an entire week to pet-sit, because they welcome the opportunity to get away from noisy dormitories and study in a quiet private house.

> Finding a really good pet-sitter who can be trusted with your puppy and your home takes a lot of effort; but once you find one, it's an easy row to hoe from there on after the sitter stays the first time or two and gets used to the routine. A good sitter is worth the money and peace of mind.

How do we select a good kennel?

A kennel might be a good way to see that your puppy is cared for if you can't find someone you trust to keep him safe in your absence. Be sure to get more than one recommendation before handing over your puppy to any kennel. Ask other dog owners and your veterinarian or someone on staff at your local humane society for recommendations.

Once you find a place that comes highly recommended by more than one source, check it out yourself. A good kennel will welcome a visit from a potential new client.

Make sure the kennel is clean and that the dogs have a comfortable place to stay. Ask if the facility has someone there overnight to watch the dogs; some kennels cannot afford to pay for overnight staff, but I'd certainly want someone around who can take action if there were a fire or if my puppy became ill overnight. Look at the layout of the place to see if it is designed to give dogs maximum attention. I heard about one kennel that has the dogs' quarters in a semicircle around an open office, so the staff can keep an eye on the dogs at all times.

Also ask how often the dogs are exercised, inquire if anyone plays with them and how often, and get specifics on the feeding schedule. A good kennel will feed your dog the same food you do or that you provide, and will follow the dog's usual feeding schedule. You also should be able to bring with your dog familiar items, such as his bed and favorite toys. Ask if the kennel has a veterinarian on call at all times and what its emergency procedures are.

Take your puppy to visit the kennel at least once — and preferably more often — before leaving him there. However, before you leave your dog at a kennel or even visit, make sure he has had all the necessary immunizations (a good kennel will request evidence of this), and have your veterinarian administer a vaccine to prevent kennel cough (a potentially serious infectious respiratory disease), which is a risk anywhere there are many dogs.

After you leave your puppy in the care of a kennel, pay careful attention to how he acts when you pick him up. If he had a pleasant stay, the kennel should report that he ate well and his weight should be the same as when you left him. He'll look good and act like his usual self. If you think you'll need to use the place again in the future, take him back a few days after his first stay: If he liked the kennel, he'll enter willingly; if he didn't, he'll balk.

I'd be especially concerned if the dog looks poorly, has lost weight, and doesn't seem himself. It could signal poor care — or it could mean that your puppy just can't adjust to kennel life.

What to Tell the Pet-Sitter

Leaving written information for your puppy's sitter is imperative. A sitter can't possibly remember every little detail you give verbally. If you have a computer, type out the basics, save it, then update as necessary in the future and print it out each time the sitter comes to the house. Here's the basic information you should leave:

- Puppy's name
- Feeding schedule
- "Bathroom" schedule
- Usual exercise schedule (walks, play sessions, etc.)
- Favorite toys and games and treats
- Any necessary medication instructions (review administration of any medication with the sitter before you leave)
- A few notes about any kind of "mischief" the puppy tends to get into and how to prevent it, such as "Keep laundry room door shut to keep puppy out"
- Extra safety precautions, such as "No rawhide unless you supervise"
- The address where you will be, and the phone number, in case of an emergency
- The names and phone numbers of three family members or good friends and neighbors who could help in case of an emergency with the puppy or your house, or in case someone else needs to take over should your pet-sitter become ill or have an emergency
- Your regular veterinarian's name, address, and phone number, and hours when the clinic is open
- The name, address, and phone number of the local emergency clinic you would use when your veterinarian's office is closed
- A letter addressed "To Whom It May Concern." Here's what I say in this letter: *(Pet-sitter's name) has permission to authorize any treatment that a veterinarian deems necessary for my dog, (dog's name). I will bear full financial responsibility.*
  If appropriate, add:
  My puppy is up-to-date on his vaccinations. His veterinarian is (veterinarian's name, address, and phone number).

If your puppy has any kind of medical condition a veterinarian should know about, put it in the letter, and date the letter and sign it. Keep in mind that if a sitter has to take your puppy to an emergency clinic, the veterinarian on duty will need a history.

My regular veterinarian would never require such a letter, but I once heard about an emergency clinic that refused to treat an injured dog without authorization from the owner, who could not readily be reached.

part ②

Tools and Training Guide

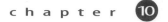
Tools for Controlling Your Puppy

reating a space for your puppy; investing in a bed; obtaining equipment such as baby gates, collar, and leash; and establishing a regular schedule are all strategies that will enable you to control your puppy now and help him develop good habits. The earlier your puppy can become accustomed to his surroundings and belongings the more secure he will be.

Give Your Dog a Space

Initially, you'll want the puppy confined to a designated area in the house. If he's left loose, he might get hurt while you are out or if you are not home to keep an eye on him. Trainers say that giving puppies too much freedom too soon is a major reason that puppies get into mischief and develop bad habits. Instead of letting a puppy run amok, it is preferable to confine him to his space and give him access only to the objects you provide for him, such as chews.

As an example of just how a puppy can go wild when given more freedom than he's used to, I'll tell you what mine did. We live in a town house and have a small fenced-in backyard. Most of the exercise Butch gets is during walks on a leash or playing fetch with a ball in the house. One week when I had to go out of town, I left the dog at my parents' — who are experienced dog owners. They have a larger home and a fenced-in backyard.

Leave on a radio or television in your puppy's space when you go out. This will help mask outdoor sounds that could either frighten the puppy or prompt him to bark.

Despite my mother's watchful eye, the dog managed to empty all the trash cans in the bathrooms, pulled things out of cupboards she says she'd forgotten she had, and dragged a giant branch from the yard into the house and chewed it up under the dining room table. The day I came home, the dog had already managed to get ahold of a downed bird in the yard, which he brought into the house. Feathers were still flying when I got there. My folks are fond of Butch and were in good humor about his antics, but I think they were very glad to see their "granddog" go home. The dog just wasn't used to having this much room to romp.

Choose the space wisely. If you choose a space that is very pleasant, and where your dog has plenty of room to move about, you can use that space far into the future as necessary. Sometimes, dogs need to be confined due to illness or injury. If your puppy becomes used to a space now, he will more readily accept confinement to that space later in life.

Even though your puppy has his own space, you'll want to have him out and about the house with you as much as possible and to sleep with you or your children in their rooms at night. (Some trainers would argue with the latter advice, but I believe this is how a puppy becomes an integral part of the household and a real family member.) Periodically confine him to his space, however, so he continues to accept it, just in case you ever need to confine him in the future.

Selecting a Room

The type of space you select will depend on your dog and the design of your house. I have always preferred using the kitchen. Kitchens tend to be one of the warmest rooms in the house and generally are easy to puppy-proof. They are the place where families tend to congregate, which is where your pet should be. They usually have floors that are easy to clean in case of an accident. By using a room such as the kitchen, the puppy is confined but still has room to move around. If you do not want your dog loose in the house for hours at a time, even when he is older, I think it is preferable to have him confined to a room where he can move about, stretch his legs, or lie on his side with his legs straight out if he wants to, instead of confining him to a cage, which is discussed below.

If your kitchen is too tiny even for a puppy, or if it is so open that you cannot confine the puppy, even with the extra-wide baby gates that are available, you'll have to be creative.

Other rooms and spaces in the house you could use for your puppy might be a large bathroom, a hallway, or a pantry. Whatever room you choose, block in the puppy with baby gates so he can see out, preferably into other rooms of the house.

Never, ever lock your puppy in a small room, with the door closed and the lights out, or keep your puppy in a dark, damp basement. This is an unpleasant life for a puppy. Puppies can become quite scared if they cannot see out.

The kitchen often makes an excellent puppy "space."

Cages

Another choice for a puppy space is a cage, usually referred to as a crate. If your puppy came from a breeder who already trained her to become accustomed to a cage, and if the puppy seems perfectly happy in the cage, this can be a good choice.

Judicious use of a cage is a good way to housebreak some dogs and provides a safe place to keep them out of mischief when owners are not home. However, some dogs will panic if locked into a cage, as though they are claustrophobic. A cage is not a place I would want to keep a dog for many hours at a time, nor would I want my dog to have to stay in a cage throughout her entire puppyhood or throughout her life every time I went out. Some people keep their dogs this way, and I wonder why they even have a dog.

Selecting a Safe Cage

If you want to cage your puppy, be sure to buy a cage that is comfortable and safe. It should be large enough for the dog to completely stand up and to lie down and stretch out on a bed within the cage. The cage should have enough room to allow food and water bowls to be placed away from the bed. It should have comfortable, solid footing and soft bedding. The cage should have no nails or edges that could injure the puppy.

There are many professionally built, wire-coated cages that are safe, and because they are wire, the dog can see out. I think these are preferable to dog "carriers," which do not provide much visibility compared with a cage. Some dogs, however, prefer a more closed environment; if this is the case, you can drape a large towel or blanket over one end of the cage, where the dog sleeps.

Top-of-the-line cages are not inexpensive; some of the smaller models cost close to $100, and large ones cost close to $200. Many can be easily folded flat for storage or travel. A good cage will last forever, so buy a well-made, high-quality model.

Make sure any cage you buy has a top that cannot be popped open from the inside if the dog knocks against it while jumping up. If you can, find a cage with extra security latches that prevent this from happening.

This story from a Baltimore breeder explains why: She had a rambunctious puppy that popped up the top of a cage, got her neck caught between the top and a side panel, and strangled to death. The dog was not a large-breed puppy — she was a tiny Boston Terrier. Security latches can prevent this kind of tragedy. Collars or halters can get hung up, so remove them before placing a puppy in a cage.

Getting a Puppy Used to a Cage

Dogs must be gradually introduced to a cage or kennel. Treats can be put into the cage to encourage the puppy to go inside. This should be done numerous times, and rather casually, before the puppy is locked in the cage. The first time you close the door, do it only for a few seconds at first, and gradually work up to minutes and beyond.

Breeders who recommend caging advise that after introducing your puppy to a cage, you should ignore any yapping that is likely to occur initially. They say the puppy should settle down after about ten minutes. If the puppy seems frantic after this period of time, I wouldn't push it — I'd remove the dog from the cage.

Assuming your puppy accepts the cage, put it in a dog-friendly room, such as the kitchen, so he can eventually "graduate" easily to a bigger space. For instance, you could keep the puppy in the cage in the kitchen, and lock him in when you have to go out for short periods of time during the first several weeks. Then, put up baby gates to confine the dog to that room, and leave open the cage door. Do this a few times when you are home before you go out and leave the dog with access to the room.

Keep the dog's bed in the cage even though the door remains open. You could put the food and water bowls either inside or outside of the cage. Puppies who like their cage will sleep in it, but they will enjoy venturing out to look around from time to time. If you want the puppy to use the cage to sleep in overnight, I'd move the cage to your bedroom at night so the puppy is with you, especially if you leave your puppy alone for several hours daily.

Baby Gates

Baby gates are one of the best investments you can make. They provide an excellent way to control puppies or dogs of any age. When you chose baby gates, be sure to select models that are safe for a young dog. Wooden gates may not be the best choice if you have a chewer on your hands; the dog could end up ingesting splinters. Some gates have V-shaped openings; very small dogs might be able to get their heads through and choke, so avoid this style of gate if you have a small-breed puppy.

There are a wide variety of gates made just for dogs (and available through pet supply catalogs) that are made of high-impact plastic or polypropylene instead of wood and that let a puppy see out without presenting a choking hazard. Some must be mounted to the doorway, and others do not — they can be secured with pressure. One of my favorite models is the "walk-through" style gate, which has a hand release that lets you swing it in so you can get in and out of the puppy's room easily. This gate is more expensive than a simple, wooden gate (it costs in the $40 to $50 range), but it should last for many years and is worth the investment, I think.

If you have a very large-breed puppy and an ordinary gate won't keep him in, you can buy extra-tall gates, or you can even mount two gates, one on top of another.

Baby gates are versatile. You can change their location as needed based on your puppy's behavior. For instance, your puppy may be well behaved after he graduates from the kitchen to adjoining rooms, but he may still get into dirty laundry if he goes into one of the bedrooms. Use baby gates to block off the hallway to the bedrooms. If the dog sleeps in your bedroom but you are worried he'll wander off while you are asleep and get into mischief or hurt himself, put up a baby gate in your bedroom doorway to keep the puppy in.

Exercise Pens

An alternative method of confining a puppy that I like is an indoor exercise pen or puppy play pen which is really much like a cage but usually larger. This may be a good choice if the design of your house makes it impossible to confine the puppy to a room with baby gates, and you do not want to use a cage.

Generally, these pens are made of heavy-gauge wire, come in a variety of sizes, and may even have doors. Many have panels you can add or remove to change their size, so they are versatile.

For the puppy, a pen can provide a room within a room. If you get one large enough for your breed of dog, there should be plenty of room to move about, a place for a bed, and newspaper if you are paper training. Pens can be purchased through pet supply catalogs. The price varies with the size; but one with six panels, each four feet wide and 36 inches high, costs under $90.

Beds

If your puppy becomes used to sleeping on her bed while she's in her space, you can use the bed to help control her in other rooms or when you take her on trips. For instance, if you take your puppy to bed with you at night and place her bed on top of yours or on the floor next to yours, chances are she will sleep on her own bed, instead of sleeping on your sheets. If you take your puppy with you to visit relatives, she is more likely to settle down for a nap when she is tired if her familiar bed is available.

To encourage use of her bed on command, teach her the phrase "Go to bed" or "Get in your bed," and follow with verbal praise such as "Good girl!" simply by saying this phrase every time she goes to her bed, or you put her there. Never put her in her bed harshly or use her bed as punishment. You want her to always associate her bed with something positive.

A dog's bed does not have to be fancy. It should protect the dog from cold, hard floors. It should be located in a place that is free from drafts. You can use a cardboard box with a thick quilt or blanket, if necessary. Make sure the box has no staples or anything else that could injure the dog. Blankets or quilts should not have loose strings or fringe, which the dog might ingest. This type of bedding may be a good temporary choice if you have a chewer or digger on your hands. I'll never forget the time one of my puppies tore up a large dog bed filled with compacted bits of foam; when I got home, it looked like there'd been an explosion in a foam rubber factory.

When you can, however, invest in a good bed for your dog that can be transported easily from room to room or on trips if you plan to take your dog along. Remember, too, that puppies grow rapidly, so buy one that will be big enough when the dog reaches her adult size. Larger dogs especially like to stretch out on their sides with legs straight out, and they should have a bed large enough to accommodate this position.

There are a wide variety of dog beds available in pet stores and catalogs. One of the nicest selections of beds I've seen for large-breed dogs is in the *Doctors Foster & Smith* catalog. (Addresses appear in the Appendix.) Select a bed that looks sturdy (which should last for years) and that is washable or has a washable cover. Many beds for larger dogs are filled with cedar, which is supposed to help control odor and, say some people, repel fleas. If you buy one of these, be sure the cedar is well enclosed in a bag within the bed and that it's not loose. Otherwise, you won't be able to wash the bedcover. Other beds are filled with poly/cedar combinations.

For very tiny dogs that like to curl up, I recommend a bed that is actually designed for cats. Called the Kitty Sleeper, it's made of a slightly fuzzy material and is a donut shape. It is flat in the middle and has thick, rolled sides. I have not been able to find this type of bed in local pet stores; I found mine in the *R. C. Steele* pet catalog. It is not in all the catalogs this company sends, so you may have to ask for what you want. I like it because it is a nice place for a little dog to snuggle, and it conforms to the dog's position. The bottom is not well padded, however, so I place it on top of a blanket. Unfortunately, the model I have says "hand wash," but I put it in the washer on the delicate cycle and line dry it. So far, so good . . .

If your puppy becomes used to sleeping on her own bed at home, she will be more likely to sleep on it in other places, too.

I do not like beds that are shaped into the form of a dog bed from solid pieces of foam with removable covers; I've always found it difficult to get the covers back on after washing. And, despite the cover, the foam always seems to get dirty.

Collars and Leashes

It is important that you purchase a good-quality collar for your puppy right away. It is essential in training, and it will provide a place to attach her identification tag. You may also want to purchase a halter to use when walking the dog if you have a small-breed dog that can easily slip out of a collar.

A collar should be just large enough for you to get two fingers underneath. A halter should fit similarly: You should just be able to get a couple fingers underneath. Some collars are made of leather and some of nylon. Some owners prefer leather if they have a long-haired dog because it may cause less matting than flat, nylon collars. Leather collars can stretch, however, so you'll have to check the size; and they will need to be cleaned and oiled to prevent cracking.

A good-quality collar and leash are essential.

Make sure the buckle on the halter or collar is secure and won't easily come undone. I've seen some collars with weak hardware that bends; avoid this type. More on collars (including training collars, such as the choke), halters, and a special training system called Gentle Leader for fractious dogs appears in chapter 8, Training Frustrations.

Frequently check the fit of your puppy's collar and halter to make sure they haven't gotten too small. Puppies grow rapidly, so unless you have a very small breed of dog that isn't going to grow much larger, expect to adjust the collar often; you probably will have to replace it with a larger one before your dog becomes full-grown. There was a news report in my area about a dog that had to have a collar removed surgically, because the owner had let it get so tight it became imbedded in the dog's neck!

Order identification tags for your dog's collar or halter that give the dog's name, your address, and phone number. The puppy's rabies vaccine tag also should be attached. You can purchase tags from pet catalogs, some pet stores, and veterinary offices.

There are a wide variety of leashes available. Flat, nylon leashes are popular, but I've found some of them are slick and hard to hang onto. Consider investing in a good-quality leather leash to use for walking your dog. You may want a longer one for training; these often are made of nylon, but you won't be using it as often as the walking leash. Routinely check any leashes you have to make sure the clasps that attach to your dog's collar or leash are in good condition and that there are no frayed places. If there are, replace the equipment.

Schedules

Puppies that have their basic needs met are more likely to be well behaved. A puppy that is hungry will pester her owner for food. A puppy that needs to expend energy, but hasn't been given the opportunity, is more likely to get into mischief. So plan a schedule for your puppy.

Feeding times should be consistent. Owners should adjust their schedules or make other arrangements to ensure their puppies are fed on time — aim for feeding within the same hour for each meal, each day. Even if you "free feed" your puppy by leaving out dry food at all times, you'll probably want to supplement with a little canned food at a regular time once or twice daily.

If you are housebreaking your puppy instead of paper training her, you also should adjust your schedule or make arrangements to make your plan work.

Seeing to it that puppies get the exercise and socialization they need can sometimes present a more difficult problem, considering the hectic schedules that characterize so many of our lives. You may not be able to walk the dog or have your play session everyday at the same time; but do make sure that each and everyday, your puppy gets attention that goes beyond the interaction that takes place at feeding and "bathroom" time.

If you miss your usual walk, for instance, make it a point to play a longer game of fetch in the backyard or indoors with your puppy later.

If you know your puppy will be alone all evening because the family is going out to dinner, plan a good walk with her before you go out. If I think my dog has had a very boring day because of my schedule, I sometimes take him for a drive around the neighborhood in the evening. By forming the habit of incorporating special time with your puppy into your life, you guarantee that she will receive the attention she needs and deserves.

chapter 11

Training Basics

You may not realize it, but you've been training your puppy from the first minute you got her. Each time you say her name and she moves from where she is to where you are, she is learning the command "Come." You just have to add the word "Come" routinely so she makes the association. When you encourage her to go along with you as you walk from one room of the house to the other, you are setting the stage to teach her the command "Heel." Be sure to use the command words when you have the opportunity. If you combine this effort with some formal training, your dog will learn quickly; but you have to keep it up — you must be consistent and persistent.

Opinions vary about when to start formal training. By formal, I simply mean setting aside a few minutes here and there, totaling about ten to 20 minutes daily to work with your puppy. You might work with the dog five minutes in the morning, five more minutes after lunch, and five minutes in the evening.

Some trainers say not to start until a puppy is about six months of age; others say to start immediately. I think it depends on your dog; sooner probably is better than later as long as you tailor the training to your puppy.

Be aware that some puppies just don't have the concentration power to learn "Sit," "Stay," "Come," and "Heel." Experiment. As soon as your dog seems capable, begin in earnest. Special training problems are addressed in chapter 8, Training Frustrations; but here are some tips to help you successfully teach your puppy the basics:

■ **Have one person in the family conduct the training.** Even if everyone in the family is using the same verbal commands, their timing will be slightly different, which could confuse the dog. It should be someone who is patient. Have other family members work with the dog later, after her learning is well under way. Just be sure everyone in the family is using the same commands. If the puppy seems confused or backslides when more than one person works with her, return to having only one family member conduct the training.

■ **Use positive reinforcement.** Reward the dog as she learns, and *never punish or become unpleasant when she doesn't catch on right away. If the dog associates obedience with something pleasant, she is more likely to obey. If she associates obedience with scolding, she won't learn as well.* Training is not the time to issue the word "No." "No" should be used only to correct inappropriate behavior. A puppy that doesn't catch on right away to training is not misbehaving. She just hasn't yet learned what you want her to do.

Use treats to encourage your puppy. Don't use them every single time, however; otherwise you'll find yourself with a dog that only obeys when you have a treat in hand! You might, for instance, use a treat frequently as you first start to teach the dog, then gradually ask the dog to do more before she gets a treat.

■ **Teach one command at a time.** Move on to an additional command only after the dog has caught on well to the first.

■ **Keep your voice cheerful.** Some dogs respond best to a very playful, coaxing voice, whereas others respond better to a slightly stern — but still pleasant — voice. Again, experiment to see which tone of voice gets you the best response.

■ **Keep your sense of humor.** Puppies are distracted easily and can try your patience. Focus on your puppy's accomplishments, no matter how small they are, and enjoy your time with her. She won't be a puppy for long, after all.

■ **Train in various places.** All the commands can be practiced in the house, in the yard, or with the dog on leash at a neighborhood park. If you vary the places you train your dog, more likely she'll learn to obey wherever you are. Training her in different places also will help socialize your puppy.

■ **Train your puppy as you play.** For instance, if you are playing fetch with a ball, ask your puppy to "Sit" before throwing the ball. Say "Come" as she returns with the ball. This reinforces your formal sessions, and since playtime is fun, it will help the dog learn to associate obedience with something pleasant.

■ **Integrate training into daily life.** As soon as your dog learns a command, begin using it routinely, not just during training sessions, and continue to reward the dog appropriately. Say "Heel" as you go from the kitchen to the living room, for example, and reward her when she obeys. If you take her for a ride in the car, ask her to "Sit" or tell her "Down" if you have been teaching her these commands, then praise her as soon as she takes the correct position. Integrating commands into daily life as soon as possible will help ensure that your dog learns to listen in all types of situations, not just during training sessions.

■ **Do not expect a dog of any age to obey every command every single time.** Dogs are living creatures, not robots. They have good days and not-so-good days, just as people do. Sometimes they concentrate better than others. This is why keeping your dog on a leash anytime she is not in a fenced-in yard or in the house is imperative. Most dogs can, however, learn to obey commands most of the time if you are persistent with training.

Communicating with Your Puppy

Puppies develop an amazing "vocabulary." They learn to understand words and phrases we say in a certain tone of voice in association with certain settings, our moods, and actions. If we usually pick up the puppy's leash each time we brightly say "Let's go for a walk!" the puppy soon learns what this means and usually will wiggle his tail and head for the door. If we say "Let's go for a walk" in a deadpan tone of voice while we're going to bed, the puppy won't know what we are talking about. Following are just a few of the words and phrases that dogs learn to recognize. Keep track of the ones your puppy learns to recognize, and you'll be surprised at how long the list grows.

Word or phrase	Setting/Owner Action
"Dinnertime!"	In the kitchen
"Let's go for a ride in the car!"	Pick up keys
"Go get your ball."	Playful tone of voice
"Let's get a bath!"	Walk into bathroom
"Do your business."	Walk toward the back door
"Get in your bed."	Your bedtime routine
"Your ball's upstairs."	Playful voice, pointing up
"Get a drink."	End of play session

"Sit"

Some puppies will learn to sit if you simply hold a piece of food just above their mouths. As they reach up for the food, they sit. If your dog will sit this way, say the word "Sit" as soon as his rump goes down. After he does this several times, try using the word without the treat and see if he obeys.

The other way to teach "Sit" is with a collar and leash. Stand next to the dog so that he is on your left and as though you are about to take him for a walk, holding the leash in both hands. Gather up the leash so there's not much slack. Gently pull up on the dog's neck, and very gently push on the dog's rear end, while saying "Sit." The second the dog sits, issue a treat and lots of verbal praise.

Another approach to teaching "Sit" is to simply lift the dog's chin with one hand. If necessary, push under the back legs into the "Sit" position, or *gently* push down on the dog's rear end.

"Stay"

Ask your puppy to "Sit." Show the dog the palm of your hand while saying "Stay," which provides visual reinforcement to the command. Take one step back. If he doesn't move, even if it's only for a second, he's learning! *Issue a reward before he has a chance to move.* Repeat, and gradually take a few more steps away from the dog. As your puppy learns, ask him to "Sit" and then walk around him as well as away from him. Expect it to take time for your dog to learn to stay put for very long.

"Down"

Ask your dog to "Sit." Then get on the floor with the dog and say "Down" as you gently pull out the puppy's front feet so that he has to lie down. As soon as you get him down, praise him. "Down" can be a bit harder to teach some dogs, because you are asking the dog to get into a position where he'll feel he has less control. You are essentially asking him to succumb. Be patient.

If your dog is an especially cooperative pupil, you may be able to teach him "Down" just by holding a treat on the floor under his nose.

"Come"

Along with "Stay," this is probably the most important command you can teach your dog. If he learns to always come when you call instead of dashing off toward a street, it could save his life, so work on this command a lot.

Always reward your dog, at first with treats and later with a combination of treats and pats on the head, every single time he comes to you throughout his life! Never, ever call your dog to you and scold him, so he doesn't learn to associate "Come" with a negative experience. If you need to correct your dog, go to him instead.

If your puppy has readily been coming to you in the house when you call his name, you're off to a good start. Instead of using his name, practice saying "Come" in the same tone of voice. Then incorporate "Come" into your formal training sessions.

If your puppy doesn't so readily come, put him on a long leash. Ask him to "Sit" and "Stay." Walk away, turn to face the dog, then say "Come." Tug on the leash a little to help show him what you want. Reward him, then repeat, repeat, repeat. When you think he's caught on, practice without the leash in the house.

"Heel" and "Stop"

Put on the dog's collar and attach a short leash. Have the dog sit by your left side. You should hold the leash in both hands. The handle end will be in your right hand; I like to put my wrist through the handle loop, then grasp the part of the leash just below in my palm. Your left hand will be about midway down the leash, holding the leash with your palm down.

Begin walking, and the second you step off, say "Heel." You may have to give a little tug to let her know she's supposed to go along. Once your puppy gets the idea, walk for several feet, then stop. Say "Stop" as you do. Keep practicing. Start throwing in right turns, then left turns. Teaching your dog to stop could save her life, and I think a dog responds more quickly to "Stop" than to "Come," which requires an additional movement — stopping and then moving toward you.

From the beginning, strive to get your dog to walk with her nose barely in front of your leg. A dog tugging ahead, pulling the owner, is one of the most common problems experienced with "Heel," because the dog has not learned from the beginning to stay back when walking next to her owner. Making frequent turns helps keep your dog's attention, which may prevent tugging ahead. If not, try this: Issue a sharp, quick jerk release of the collar when she tugs to let her know this is unacceptable. I also say "Wait!" at the same time.

Never, ever jerk so hard that it pulls your puppy's head to the side, the head up, and certainly never so hard it pulls your puppy off her feet. Just because some trainers do this doesn't mean it's right. You could injure a dog, especially a puppy.

Pay special attention to crossing driveways within communities and streets. Routinely stop at a sidewalk before entering a street, have the dog sit (if it isn't summer and the pavement isn't scorching hot), then

Teaching your puppy not to cross a street without you could save his life.

proceed across. If your dog wanders toward the street while you are walking her, let her get to the curb, then issue a sharp jerk and a "No!" to teach her she is not to go near the street unless she is on "Heel" next to you. This lesson, like "Come," could be lifesaving for your dog.

There are a couple other commands you can teach in addition to "Heel" that will make walking with your dog more pleasant for you both. Although you'll want your dog to obey you most times you are walking her on the leash, let her know there are times she can be "at ease," which means she is allowed to depart from your side (still on leash) to do her "business" and generally sniff around at her leisure. I use the word "Okay." This indicates to my dog that he no longer has to heel. I also say "Show me!" which means the dog gets to choose where we go. He pulls ahead on these ventures, but enjoys leading me here and there. Usually, he wants to go up the street to see his friend Murphy, a Golden Retriever. This kind of variation makes walks more fun for the dog.

"Roll Over"

This isn't considered as important a command as "Come" or "Stay," but it is handy to have a dog that will roll over if you want to check for fleas or ticks on the tummy or get a larger dog into a position that may make it easier for you to clip his nails. Start teaching "Roll Over" only after your dog has mastered "Down." Hold a treat in one hand on the floor, and move it in an arc position in front of the dog's face, as if to signal "roll over," and with the other hand, roll the dog over to his side.

If he's very cooperative, you may be able to roll him over all the way, from one side to the other, the first time. If he balks, make your goal just to roll him on his side. Slowly work up to rolling him completely from one side to the other. Give a treat the moment the dog acquiesces to your moving his body. If the dog is too big for you to roll over with one hand, enlist the assistance of a helper. After doing this several times, many dogs will catch on and begin to roll themselves.

Combine the Commands

When your puppy has mastered each command, start using more than one command during each training session. Add one at a time; when the puppy has mastered two, add a third.

To see just how well your dog is learning, conduct off-leash training sessions indoors to see if he obeys. Outdoors, you can test the dog by using a longer leash and keeping it slack to see if he obeys without pressure from the leash.

Hand Signals

Teaching your dog hand signals is fun, and it is easier than you think. Quite inadvertently, I taught my dog to lie down when I tap my fist to my chest. I noticed that I'd been making this gesture, without realizing it, when I was teaching him the verbal command "Down." A more common hand signal for "Down," however, is showing the dog your hand with the palm facing the floor. I use an upward hand motion for "Sit." You can make up your own signals to go with each verbal command. Just use them as you teach your dog the verbal commands. After he's listening well to you verbally, try using only the hand signals.

Training Classes and Professional Trainers

Consider seeking outside help for training your puppy if (1) you've never had a dog before and don't feel confident teaching your puppy; (2) you have tried yourself, but do not feel you are making progress; or (3) your dog is having special, serious behavior problems that you can't seem to resolve yourself, such as aggressive behavior.

If any one of these situations applies to you, enroll in a dog obedience class. Your local humane society or veterinarian can make a recommendation. Many localities offer dog obedience classes. Attending a dog obedience class also is a great way to meet new people. Be sure your veterinarian says your puppy has had all the necessary immunizations and that it is safe to expose her to other dogs. A reputable trainer will ask about this. The cost of obedience classes will vary depending on where you live. In my area, they run just under about $20 per class and usually are offered in a series of eight classes.

Another option is to hire a private trainer to work with you and your puppy. If you want to go this route, select a trainer *very carefully.* Anyone can call himself a dog trainer. Although there are many fine trainers around, there also are trainers who use severe, inhumane methods and unnecessarily use negative instead of positive reinforcement. Expect to pay at least twice as much for private training compared with group classes; but this, too, will vary depending on where you live and which trainer you use.

Again, ask your local humane society, or get a recommendation from your veterinarian. When interviewing trainers, ask if they use positive or negative reinforcement. Ask, too, for references from several clients; a good trainer will be glad to provide names. Be sure to call each reference and follow up. If a dog owner doesn't have much to say about a trainer, beware. Of course, references are of limited value, because a trainer is going to give you names of people he thinks will say good things about him, but the process may provide some useful information.

Be sure to ask about payment. If a trainer wants money up front for more than one session, be leery. You may not like the trainer after one session, in which case you should not use that trainer again.

Some trainers teach the dog for you. Some even take dogs to their homes or training facility to work on special problems. I recently heard about a man who had a dog with separation anxiety. Every time the owner went out, the dog tore up the house. The man hired a trainer who took the dog to his own home. After a few weeks of gradual conditioning to get the dog used to being alone, the trainer "cured" the dog. The animal could be left alone for several hours without destroying anything. But guess what? The first time the dog was back in his owner's home alone, he went wild again and dug out a huge hole in the drywall! The problem here is obvious. The dog had been conditioned to stay alone in the trainer's house, but not in his owner's. Hire a trainer who teaches *you* how to train your dog.

Appendix

Suppliers

Premier Pet Products
527 Branchway Road
Richmond, VA 23236
(804) 379-4702 or (800) 933-5595
Gentle Leader Head Collar System (wholesale only)

Safe Brands Corporation
727 South 13th Street
Omaha, NE 68102
For product information: (800) 289-7234
To learn what stores in your area sell Sierra: (888) 88-SIERA
SIERRA Antifreeze-Coolant

Organizations

National Association of Professional Pet-Sitters
1200 G Street, NW, Suite 760
Washington, DC 20005
(202) 393-3317
Fax: (202) 393-0336
Web: www.petsitters.org
Pet-Sitter referral: (800) 296-PETS

National Dog Registry
P.O. Box 116
Woodstock, NY 12498
(914) 679-BELL
(800) 637-3647

National Pet Protection Network
494 Sheridan Blvd., Suite 200A
Lakewood, CO 80226
(303) 922-0098

Veterinary Pet Insurance
4175 East LaPalma Avenue, Suite 100
Anaheim, CA 92807
(800) USA-PETS
E-mail: vsapets@primenet.com
Web: www.petinsurance.com

Pet Catalogs

The following catalogs offer a wide variety of pet products including dog
coats and sweaters, food bowls, crates and cages, kennels, odor elimina-
tors, health care products, and collars and leashes.

Doctors Foster & Smith Inc.
2253 Air Park Road
P.O. Box 100
Rhinelander, WI 54501
(800) 826-7206
Free catalog

Omaha Vaccine Company
P.O. Box 7228
Omaha, NE 68107
(800) 367-4444

R. C. Steele
1989 Transit Way
Box 910
Brockport, NY 14420
(800) 872-3773
Fax: (716) 637-8244
Requires $50 minimum order

Recommended Reading

Dog Behavior and Training: Veterinary Advice for Owners by Lowell Ackerman, Gary Landsberg, and Wayne Hunthausen (Neptune City, NJ: TFH Publications, 1996). Veterinarians give their views on dog behavior and training in this handy book.

The Dog Owner's Home Veterinary Handbook by Delbert C. Carlson, D.V.M., and James M. Giffin, M.D. (New York, NY: Howell Book House, 1992). A veterinarian and a physician have teamed up to write a book that I think is a definite must for anyone with a dog. It's easy to read and will give you a clear idea of when you can take care of a problem at home, and when you need to call the veterinarian. It's my all-time favorite in pet care medical books.

The Dog Who Loved Too Much by Nicholas Dodman (New York: Bantam Books, 1996). This is a good read for anyone who is interested in dogs. Dr. Dodman, a veterinarian and animal behavior specialist, also gives valuable insight into dog behavior and solutions for behavior problems.

Dr. Pitcairn's Complete Guide to Natural Health for Dogs and Cats by Richard Pitcairn, D.V.M., and Susan Hubble Pitcairn (Emmaus, PA: Rodale Press, 1995). This book is a good option for dog owners who want to use a more natural approach to pet care. It includes home-cooked recipes for your dog's diet.

Good Dog, Bad Dog: Dog Training Made Easy by Mordecai Siegal and Matthew Margolis (New York, NY: Henry Holt & Co., 1991). You can depend on any book by Mordecai Siegal and/or Matthew Margolis to provide a sound, humane approach to dog training.

I Just Got a Puppy: What Do I Do? by Matthew Margolis and Mordecai Siegal (New York, NY: Fireside, 1992). Another helpful book by two of my favorite dog experts.

UC Davis Book of Dogs: A Complete Medical Reference Guide for Dogs and Puppies by the School of Veterinary Medicine Staff and Mordecai Siegal (New York, NY: HarperCollins Publishers, Inc., 1995). The staff at the University of California, Davis, and Mordecai Siegal, a top-notch animal health writer, provide an in-depth view of dogs's health problems. Up-to-date treatment information is included.

Index

Illustrations are indicated by page numbers in *italics*.

Bowls, 59–61, *60*
Breeders, 145
Brushes, *108*
Brushing, 108–10

C

Caging. *See* Crating
Carlson, Delbert, 82
Carpet
  discoloration of, 34
  urine odors in, 29–30
Car travel, 97–99
Catalogs and suppliers, 175, 176
Cats
  chasing, 11–12
  eating food for, 58–59
  litter boxes for, 63–64, *64*
Charging, at guests, 134–35
Chewing, 2–6
Chews, 17–19
Children, and puppies, 27–28, 39, 132
Chocolate, 101
Choke collars, 119–20
Coats (garment), 96–97, *96*
Coats (puppies')
  brushing, 108–10
  burrs in, 110–11
  discolored, 107
  dry and scaly, 107–8
  mats in, 111
Collars, *162*
  anti-barking, 128–30
  for behavior correction, 119–22, *122*
  fit of, 162

slipping out of, 118–19
Combs, 108–9
Come command, 11, 125, 169–70
Commands. *See also specific commands*
  to encourage bed use, 160
  for housetraining, 24
  for play, 38
  teaching, 123–24, 125, 165–67
  for walking, 40
Companions. *See* Playmates
Coprophagia, 63–64
Coronavirus, 68
Crating
  for housetraining, 24
  introducing puppies to, 158
  for misbehavior, 4–5
  selecting crate, 157–58
  and separation anxiety, 6–7
  for travel, 97, 101
Crying, 136–37

D

Dandruff, walking, 81
Dentabone, 114
Dental care, 113–14
Dermatitis, flea allergy, 80–81
Diarrhea
  causes of, 33
  cleaning up, 34
Diet. *See* Food; Vitamins
Digestive upsets, 33–34
Digging, 8, *8*, 92–93
Diseases. *See* Vaccinations; *specific diseases*
Distemper, 68

Parainfluenza, 68
Parvovirus, 42, 68
Paws, cleaning, 45
Pens
  indoor, 159–60
  outdoor, 49
Pet insurance, 82–84
Pet-sitters
  choosing, 146–48
  information for, 151
  training, 148–49
Pills
  administering, 71–72, *71*
  dividing, 72–73
Pitcairn, Richard, 80
Pitcairn, Susan Hubble, 80
Play
  biting during, 38–39
  fetch, 37–38, 43
  in food and water bowls, 60–61
  rough, 39
  training during, 167
  tug of war, 40
Playmates, 14, 44, 140, 143, *143*
Poison control center, 92
Poisons
  antifreeze, 93–94
  chocolate, 101
  houseplants, 92–93
  on lawns, 62
  toilet bowl cleaners, 102
Polsky, Richard H., 129, 130
Positive conditioning, 10, 13,
  166

Preventive health care, 70, 72. *See
  also* Vaccinations
Program flea control, 77

R
Rabies, 68
Record keeping, 89
Relocating, without puppies, 141–42
Rewards, 10. *See also* Positive con-
  ditioning; Treats
Rippey, Sandy, 110
Roll over command, 171–72

S
Safety
  loss prevention, 87–92
  poison prevention, 92–94, 101,
    102
  tips for, 102
  during travel, 97–101
  and weather, 94–97
Scabies, 81
Scat Mat, 13
Scent glands, 34–35
Schedules, 163–64
Scratching, on walls, 5–6. *See also*
  Itching
Separation anxiety, 2, 5–7, 128
Shampoo, 106
Shedding, 36, 109
Shedding blade, *78*, 109
Shivering, 95–97
Shock collars, 129–30
Shoes, owners', 46
Shots, 42, 67–70, 76

V

Vaccinations, 42, 67–70, 76
Veterinarians, choosing, 65–66
The Veterinarian's Encyclopedia of Animal Behavior (Beaver), 30–31, 47
Veterinary Pet Insurance (VPI), 82–83, 176
Vitamins, 55, 56
Vomiting, 61
VPI, 82–83, 176

W

Walking
  and crossing streets, 170–71, *171*
  by dog walkers, 140, 142
  and pulling ahead, 119–21, 170

  sniffing during, 40–41, *41*
Water
  bowls for, 59, *60*
  playing in, 61
  while crating, 24
Weather
  and housetraining, 26–27
  protection from, 94–97
Weight, excess, 58
Whining, 136–37
Worms
  preventing, 70
  sources of, 42, 63, 79

Y

Yelling, at puppies, 139–40

Other Storey Titles You Will Enjoy

50 Simple Ways to Pamper Your Dog, by Arden Moore. One-of-a-kind guide to grooming, exercising, feeding, and TLC with an emphasis on safety. 144 pages. Paperback. ISBN 1-58017-310-1.

The Guilt-Free Dog Owner's Guide: Caring for a Dog When You're Short on Time and Space, by Diana Delmar. Easy-to read chapters remove the anxieties associated with selecting the right dog, housebreaking, exercise, manners, behavior problems, home hazards, travel, and dog health. 180 pages. Paperback. ISBN 0-88266-575-8.

The Kitten Owner's Manual, by Arden Moore. Hundreds of practical tips on how to raise an indoor cat, as well as answers to every kitten owner's most frequently asked questions. 192 pages. Paperback. ISBN 1-58017-387-X.

Real Food for Cats: 50 Vet-Approved Recipes to Please the Feline Gastronome, by Patti Delmonte. Vet-approved, wonderfully easy recipes to make for the finicky cat. Includes tips on cat care and health, plus entertaining illustrations. Includes a special section on prescription diets for cats with special needs. 128 pages. Paperback. ISBN 1-58017-409-4.

Real Food for Dogs: 50 Vet-Approved Recipes to Please the Canine Gastronome, by Arden Moore. Fifty quick, well-balanced, vet-approved recipes provide an alternative to commercial dog food. Includes a special section on prescription diets for dogs with special needs. 128 pages. Paperback. ISBN 1-58017-424-8.

Your Puppy, Your Dog: A Kid's Guide to Raising a Happy, Healthy Dog, by Pat Storer. Both parents and children can use this thorough guide to choosing, feeding, grooming, exercising, and training a puppy. The book covers training, showing, feeding, and veterinary care. 160 pages. Paperback. ISBN 0-8266-959-1.

These books and other Storey books are available at your bookstore, farm store, garden center, or directly from Storey Publishing, 210 MASS MoCA Way, North Adams, MA 01247, or by calling 1-800-441-5700. Or visit our Web site at www.storey.com.